Rising Above the Rubbish

McDougal & Associates
Servants of Christ and Stewards of the Mysteries of God

Rising Above the Rubbish

**LIVING WORDS
FOR DEAD SITUATIONS**

BY
KAYLIN A. HAYNES

Rising Above the Rubbish
Copyright © 2017 — Kaylin A. Haynes
ALL RIGHTS RESERVED under U.S., Latin-American and International copyright conventions. No part of this book may be used or reproduced in any manner whatsoever without written permission, except in the case of brief quotations embodied in critical articles and reviews.

Unless otherwise noted, all Scripture quotations are from the *Holy Bible, New International Version*, copyright © 1973, 1978, 1984 by International Bible Society, Colorado Springs, Colorado. References marked "NKJV" are from the *Holy Bible, New King James Version* © copyright 1979, 1980, 1982 by Thomas Nelson, Inc., Nashville, Tennessee. References marked "NLT" are from *The Holy Bible, New Living Translation*, copyright © 1996, 2004, 2007 by Tyndale House Foundation, Carol Stream, IL. References marked "NASB" are from the *New American Standard Bible*, copyright © 1960, 1962, 1963, 1968, 1971, 1972, 1973, 1975, 1977 by the Lockman Foundation, La Habra, California. References marked "ASV" are from *The American Standard Version* of the Bible, Public Domain.

Published by:

McDougal & Associates
18896 Greenwell Springs Road
Greenwell Springs, LA 70739
www.thepublishedword.com

McDougal & Associates is dedicated to spreading the Gospel of the Lord Jesus Christ to as many people as possible in the shortest time possible.

ISBN 978-1-940461-62-5

Printed in the U.S., the U.K. and Australia
For Worldwide Distribution

Dedication and Acknowledgments

This book of living words is inspired by the resuscitating power of the Holy Spirit. It is dedicated:

To my Life-Giver and Gift-Giver, God the Father, Son and Holy Spirit: You are my All. Without You nothing would exist, but with You all things exist, including me. You are the reason I live, breathe, and have my being. I want to thank You for the gift of clear, expressive writing.

A gift is to give, not keep, and, because of You, I am able to use this gift to edify, encourage, teach, reprove and lead others to our ONE and only true and living Source—YOU. Through You, my Triumphant Trinity, You have created me, and You lead me, strengthen me, guide me, reprove me and instruct me. I pray to always lead others as I am led, without compromise and without apology. My commissioned call would not exist without You. I thank You for choosing me for a time such as this, to do Your greater works.

As the Father, You protect, nurture and guide me. As the Son, You saved me by Your death and resurrection. You died that I may live and have life abundantly. Your life was not Your own, and neither is mine. I surrender all to You, my Lord and Savior.

As the Holy Spirit, You are my Power, and Strength. You teach me all things, bring all things back to my remembrance and give me all wisdom and revelatory knowledge. It was through You that these writings were born. Your living waters poured tidal waves of living words into my spirit, heart and mind. Because we human beings are united in spirit, You relate to us and lead us to relate to all. You are the Great Miracle Worker. You are Universal Love.

To my parents, Marvin and Barbara Allen: I thank God for using you as my biological birth vessels. I am here because of you. Your existence is an intricate part of who I am. My mind, power, courage and personality are because of you. You are a part of all I am and do. Your encouragement over the years has been priceless. It's because of you that I never give up. You have been there when I have risen and fallen.

To my sisters, Alycia and Marva: You are not only my sisters; you are my best friends. You are always what I need when I need it.

Alycia, you have a gift of counsel. Thank you for all you have counseled me through. Your wisdom is uncanny and your love and generosity is more than this world can handle or understand.

Marva, your quiet strength has checked me numerous times and keeps me focused and humble. I catapult because of you. Thank you both for building priceless memories with me.

To my beautiful daughters, Aleah and Rayah: Thank you for pushing me to publish these writings by constantly asking me

"What are you waiting for?" You give me the same tough love I give you, and I love you and thank you for it. Continue to be the champions you expect me to be.

To every teacher I have ever had: I thank you for your individual and unique ability to reach me where I was and push me to be where I was supposed to be.

To my martial arts instructors, Grand Master Robert A. Christy Jr., Master Avery Anderson, and Sensei Randal Kiper: I thank you for the focus and discipline that has allowed me to press past the opposition in and out of the dojo. Thank you for teaching me to never give up, finish what I start and always exemplify discipline, confidence and respect.

To Kelly Haynes (Koo): You are a Soul-Friend. Thank you for always accepting the transparent me. You always accept me "as is" and love me unconditionally. You never compromised truth and always speak words of faith over me. You always tell me I can do anything. You are an eternal friend.

To Michael, My BB-LUV: Words cannot express our friendship. You have been my mirror holder, always showing me my TRUE self. I can't hide a thing from you. Our iron sharpening iron sessions helped me become transparent and taught me to live in my naked truth! Love you, BB!

To Alicia Johnson (Louise): Your unwavering friendship has been a constant during the good, the bad and the ugly seasons of life. Your mother wit and hard-core truth have made me stronger as a woman and mother. Thank you for your unconditional love and faith "claimations." They are coming to pass, as they always do.

To my spiritual father, Bishop Raymond W. Johnson: Your uncompromising teaching of the Gospel has taught, instructed and led me to never settle for mediocrity and to be willing to go against the grain for God.

Bishop, you told me one day that the dust of despair would settle, and I would stand in victory. I'm standing. Thank you for birthing Living Faith Christian Center. To all of the LFCC prayer warriors who have undergirded me in prayer, thank you.

To Darlene A. Budgewater and Roberta Diaz: Thank you for having faith in my gift and speaking life, power and wisdom into me.

Darlene, your faith, prayer and generous spirit has done more for me than words can express. You always sowed into my dreams, and I thank you and Elder B. Your bound and determined spirit inspires me.

Roberta, your gentle spirit gives me balance and teaches me the power of poise and humility. I thank you. You said you would see this book before you leave, and you have.

To my dear "Sissy" DeAndrae Parker: You are like an angel friend God just dropped into my path in perfect season. Your warrior spirit and friendship have pushed me in ways you can't imagine. I thank God for your thoughtful and generous heart. I love you.

To the Louisiana Department of Health (LDH) friends and encouragers: Your support, encouragement and special friendships have pushed me past the pity parties and propelled me to keep moving forward to complete my book. Thank you.

To my personal intercessors Shanette Buckley and Yolanda Ellis: Thank you. Your gifts have pushed me out of the comfort zones of slothfulness so I could "be about my Father's business." You are treasured blessings.

To all others who have prayed for me, sowed into me, and encouraged me: I thank you. I thank God for every stranger who crossed my path and was an angel unaware.

To Keydra Singleton (Keedy Sweedy): Thank you for pushing me to my publishing process.

To all of my Facebook friends who shared my writings: Thank you. I could not have done this without you.

> "This is what the LORD,
> the God of Israel, says:
>
> 'Write in a book all the words
> I have spoken to you.' "
>
> Jeremiah 30:2

Contents

Foundational Scriptures 15
Introduction 17

There Is Purpose in Your Process 21
Transformed to Transform 22
What's Your Name? 23
Faith Without Works Is Dead 24
He Reigns Regardless 25
Believe 26
Cycle Breaking 27
Let's Examine Ourselves 28
Slow Your Roll 29
Fight with the Right Weapons 30
Seek God and Gain All 31
The Motive Behind the Motion 32
Destiny Blockers 34
God Spoke and Created, Therefore Speak and Create 35
Meek Is Not Weak 36
Every Season Is Your Season 37
Spiritual Cancer 38
Loved to Love 39
Stay Connected to Your High Tower 41
The Pit of Spiritual Pornography 43
Don't Be a Spiritual Selfie 45

Trusting Him	46
Know His Voice and a Stranger You Will Not Follow	47
Don't Give Your Power Away	48
Breaking the Cycle of Abuse	49
Masks of Religiosity	51
Stay in Your Lane	52
Lay Aside Your Weight	53
Relationship vs. Religion	54
Press to Progress	55
Conquer Your Mountain Before It Conquers You	56
Speaking to Your Void	57
The Seasonal Pain of Parenting	59
Speak the Answer, Not the Problem	61
The After-Effects of Grief	63
The Church Needs Prayer	64
Being Prayerfully Proactive, Not Reactive	66
Warfare Prayer	67
Guard Your Gates	68
The Revelation of Rest	69
Our ALL in ALL	70
God Is Bigger than Your Battle	71
Go Deeper	72
Speak Faith; Silence Sight	73
The Ugly Duckling	74
Healing Awareness	75
Conquering ALL through Him	76
Basking in Him	77
Destiny Despair	78
Built for Battle and Destined to Win	79
Spiritual Concrete	80
Change Your World	81
Command Your Balance	82

Spiritual Drought	83
Transforming in Truth	84
You Are a Masterpiece, Not a Mistake	85
Divine Detox	86
Faith Fortress	87
Redirect and Recharge	88
Vessels of Victory	89
Cycles of Despair	90
Your Best is Yet to Come, So Fight for It.	91
The Serenity of Solitude	92
Redirect from Doubt to Faith	93
Seal, Secure and Solidify Your Blessing.	94
Birth Your Purpose	95
Our Unchanging Changer	96
The Opposition of Oppression	97
The Pains of Plan and Purpose	98
Battle Season	99
Harvest Time	100
See Yourself Magnified, Not Minuscule	101
Decisions	102
The Gift of Giving	103
Faith-Focus	104
Your Breaking Point Is Your Strongest Point	105
Raise Your Bar	106
The Power of Positivity	107
Dirty Glasses of Depression	108
Drop Your Weights	109
Love Conquers and Covers	110
Fleshly-Led vs. Spiritually-Guided	111
Deflect the Destiny Distractors	112
God Is Not a Second-Fiddle God	113
Purpose in Your Pain	114

New Day	115
There Must be Discipline Before Destiny	116
Renew and Reset	117
The Predators of Your Peace	118
The Supernatural Power of Prayer	119
No Weapon	120
Lift the Leaders and Lift the Land	121
Forgive to Be Forgiven	122
Live in Spirit and in Truth	123
The Personal Prisoner	124
Forward Faith	125
Patience through Pain	126
The War on Love	127
The Seasonal Steward	128
The Power of God's Undergirding	129
Fair-Weather Faith	130
Motive vs. Money	131
Unconditional Gratitude	132
Superficially Sick	133
Proud Purpose	134
You're God's Priority	135
He Wants Your Heart, Not Your Brain	136
The Phantom Fight	137
Leave the Pity Party	138
The Enemy of Passive Purpose	139
The Revelation of the Resurrection	140
Overcoming Your Wilderness	141
Author Contact Page	143

Foundational Scriptures

Here are some scriptures that are foundational to the teachings that follow. I urge all readers to speak, declare, believe and receive them before going forward. This will seal, secure and solidify the power of God's living promises in your life today.

Colossians 1:15-18 - *The Son is the image of the invisible God, the firstborn over all creation. For in Him all things were created: things in heaven and on earth, visible and invisible, whether thrones or powers or rulers or authorities; all things have been created through him and for Him. He is before all things, and in Him all things hold together. And He is the head of the body, the church; He is the beginning and the firstborn from among the dead, so that in everything He might have the supremacy.*

Matthew 10:8 - *Heal the sick, raise the dead, cleanse those who have leprosy drive out demons. Freely you have received; freely give.*

Matthew 19:26 - *Jesus looked at them and said, "With man this is impossible, but with God all things are possible."*

Luke 1:37 - *For with God nothing will be impossible.* (NKJV)

Romans 8:11 - *And if the Spirit of him who raised Jesus from the dead is living in you, he who raised Christ from the dead will also give life to your mortal bodies because of his Spirit who lives in you.*

Romans 10:9-13 - *If you declare with your mouth, "Jesus is Lord," and believe in your heart that God raised him from the dead, you will be saved. For it is with your heart that you believe and are justified, and it is with your mouth that you profess your faith and are saved. As Scripture says, "Anyone who believes in him will never be put to shame." For there is no difference between Jew and Gentile – the same Lord is Lord of all and richly blesses all who call on him, for, "Everyone who calls on the name of the Lord will be saved."*

Philippians 4:13 - *For I can do everything through Christ, who gives me strength.* (NLT)

Introduction

Whereever I go, I always take a few moments to observe the people in my surroundings. This helps me to stay humble. I particularly like to observe our differences. I observe differences in race, gender, age and nationality. But no matter how different we all are, no matter how rich or poor, no matter what race or nationality, old or young, and no matter what religion we are, we are all united by common bonds. We all need love, food, water, a sense of belonging and good health.

None of us wants to be lonely, hungry or sick. We all want peace, not confusion. We all want encouragement and joy, yet we, as a world, allow the superficial to blind us from the blatant truth. By carnal nature, we tend to focus on what's least important or valuable. Let's ask a simple question: If we had a loved one who was drowning, would it matter if the person there to save them was black, white, or of another race, as long as they could save them? Would it matter if they were rich or poor? Are we so superficial that we would allow our prejudices and personal hang-ups to prevent a life from being saved? Well, we have a Savior who is willing to love us all, so who are we to not be willing to do the same for others, all made in God's image just as we are? We are ONE people, united in ONE spirit, whether we accept it or not.

This book is designed to lift us above the rubbish of life's circumstances through the resuscitating power of the Holy

Spirit, who gives life to any seemingly-dead situation. If your rubbish is divorce, you will rise! If it's addiction, you will rise! If it's abuse, you will rise! If it is rejection, you will rise! If it's low self-esteem, you will rise! If it's fear, you will rise! If it's self-doubt, you will rise! If it's unforgiveness, you will rise! If it's loneliness, you will rise! If it's dead faith, you will rise!

These living words will perform spiritual resuscitation on the spiritually and emotionally dead. This book will erase the definitions of doom that life's seasons and circumstances have tried to label you with. Because the book is inspired by the power of God's Holy Spirit, the revelatory knowledge of what you are about to behold will be like fire shut up in your bones. These words will resonate within you — mind, body and spirit. As they land on the good soil of your spirit, heart, mind and body, you will begin to talk and walk by faith, not the sight of your circumstances. These words will not reinvent your spiritual wheels *per se*, but will get your spiritual wheels spinning in a different direction.

This world trains us to walk and believe by sight because we are taught to be led by our carnal senses. However, when we are reborn by the regeneration of God's Holy Spirit, we are deprogrammed and reprogrammed to walk by faith in what God's Word says, not by what our circumstances say. In a world that often operates out of religion rather than relationship, many feel lost, confused, dismayed and alone. KNOW THIS: You are not alone and have the Greatest Helper of ALL willing and able to make all things possible for you.

Your life and circumstances are about to be transformed into testimonies of victory to be shared to bless others. Dead situations are about to be resurrected into new life. God is not a massive list of do's and don'ts. He's our Unconditional Lover, Restorer, Regenerator and Reviver.

Once these words plant themselves in the soil of your entire being, you are going to see and feel the love of God. You will no longer live your life through circumstance and chance. You will live in the revelation of your purpose in God and your God-promised ordained destiny. You are about to *RISE ABOVE THE RUBBISH!*

Kaylin Haynes
Zachary, Louisiana

There Is Purpose in Your Process

The hard work, hard times, lonely years and financial famine are only seasons of faith-building and self-seeking. If you feel all alone, know that your seasons of solitude build fortitude. God wants you to know that your process is not to break you; it's to build you.

> Let's ask God to strengthen and undergird us as we press through our process. Let's ask Him to speak purpose into each step, each fall and each rise. Let's ask Him to encourage us when the process seems discouraging and impossible. Let's ask Him to strengthen us in the areas of our personal weaknesses. Work your process, and God will work His promises.

Ecclesiastes 8:6 - *For there is a proper time and procedure for every matter, though a person may be weighed down by misery.*

Transformed to Transform

Do not let the cares of life numb you. Do not let the challenges of life break you. Do not let the social ugliness you encounter change your compassion for others. Evil has a way of operating contagiously, by trying to conform and transform all things to its likeness.

The one thing the enemy wants to do is harden the heart of the believer. The coldness and carelessness of this world tries to plant in us seeds of fear, hopelessness, doubt and despair. Don't give up on kindness, love, gentleness and peace. The principles of God's Word are forever, and they will forever prevail.

> *Let's embrace life with the consciousness of knowing we ALL make a difference, we all have a purpose, and God's power is available to us—if only we would ask, believe and receive. Our individual impacts affect multitudes. Let it be for good.*

2 Corinthians 1:3-4 - *Praise be to the God and Father of our Lord Jesus Christ, the Father of compassion and the God of all comfort, who comforts us in all our troubles, so that we can comfort those in any trouble with the comfort we ourselves receive from God.*

Psalm 37:19 - *In times of disaster they will not wither; in days of famine they will enjoy plenty.*

What's Your Name?

The enemy has a way of always trying to give us a bad report. He comes to steal, kill and destroy. He strategizes through our emotional, mental and physical patterns. If he recognizes we are worriers, he brings worry. If we are easily stressed, he brings stress. If sickness is a fear, he brings reports of sickness and death. If it's lust, he brings seductive enticement. We have to know who we are and whose we are. We can't just speak religious clichés that sound good; we have to declare, by faith, what God says about us. When the enemy comes in and calls us out of our name, we must remind him of who we are through the declarations of God's unchanging Word. Your name is not Cancer; it's Healed. Your name is not Poverty, Unemployed, Confused, Abandoned, Lost, Defeated or Worthless. Your name is Abundance, Prosperity, Wealth, Wisdom, Precious, Sound Mind, Loved, Overcomer, Champion and Mr. or Ms. More Than a Conqueror!

Let's ask God to give us strength, faith and boldness when the pressures of life press hard upon us. There is power in a name. Who are you?

Isaiah 62:2 - *The Gentiles shall see your righteousness,*
And all kings your glory.
You shall be called by a new name,
Which the mouth of the LORD will name. (NKJV)

Faith Without Works Is Dead

We often face times in life when we may really need a breakthrough in health, finances or spiritual growth. Some may need divine direction regarding a critical decision. Many times we want the breakthrough without the sacrifice. We want the financial increase but not the lesson in stewardship. Some may need the weight-loss to stabilize their blood-pressure but don't want to alter the deadly diet. Some want to get fit but do not want to put in the time to exercise, eat right and get proper rest. Some want healed lungs but can't shake the cigarette habit. Some want the regenerated liver but can't seem to shake the drinking habit, to better their quality of life. Whatever it is we need, we must be willing to do our part to make it happen. Faith is great, but without works, it's dead. Put your faith with your works of discipline, self-control, obedience and life-style change, and watch the miracles, transformations and testimonies manifest.

Let's ask God to help us as we try to help ourselves. Let's ask Him to create in us a heart and mind of discipline and obedience.

Proverbs 25:28 - *A person without self-control is like a city with broken-down walls.* (NLT)

James 2:26 - *For as the body without the spirit is dead, so faith without works is dead also.* (NKJV)

He Reigns Regardless

It's amazing how this world has slowly tried to dismiss God from everything in the name of being politically correct. Sometimes it's our guilt and imperfections that try to keep God in the background, as if He can be minimized. He reigns regardless. He's been removed from corporate school prayer, holiday names are changed to discount Christ, and the pompousness of human pride is bringing moral collapse. However, when it comes to tragedy, accidents, desperation, sickness, and injuries ... everyone near and far comes together to pray collectively for God to move, and when He does we have the audacity to go back to business as usual and legislate Him away.

It's time to stand up. It's time to command and declare prayer back into our schools, universities and jobs across this nation. It's time to be world-shakers and change-makers. It's our individual obligation and commission to defend our Defender and glorify our Creator for ALL He has done, is doing and will do. He's our Healer, Provider, Heart-changer, Spirit-transformer and Deliverer.

Let's release our lives, churches, families, children, schools, universities, jobs, governments, leaders, legislators and people of influence to the fullness of God's power. Let's ask Him to come in and refill every void that we have allowed evil to fill.

---

2 Chronicles 7:14 - *Then if my people who are called by my name will humble themselves and pray and seek my face and turn from their wicked ways, I will hear from heaven and will forgive their sins and restore their land.* (NLT)

BELIEVE

Do we really realize that the lame, paralyzed, blind, sick and lost can still receive miraculous healing? Do we realize that no matter what a doctor's report says, God still reigns, and since He is the Creator, Author and Finisher of all things, He knows our bodies better than any doctor?

Doctors are great, but God is the greatest. The atmosphere is pregnant with His miraculous power across this Earth, and between each spiritual contraction comes the question: do we really believe? Our faith in His power is the antidote. He will never lose His power, but do we lose our faith? Do we really believe that dead nerves can regenerate, cancer cells can die, blood pressure can stabilize, torn limbs and tendons can reform and blind eyes can and will see?

Do churches stand in faith and anointed power to call those bound to cancer, mental illness, crutches, canes and wheelchairs to come forth for their miracle through the power of God's Holy Spirit? Or is it religious business as usual year after year? Are we afraid? The faith is in God, not us.

Let's ask God to help our unbelief, doubt and fear in all areas of our lives so we can receive more of Him and less of us. Let's pray for miraculous healing and deliverance for all who are bound by the weights and illnesses of life. Believe and receive!

Psalm 77:14 - *You are the God who performs miracles; you display your power among the peoples.*

Mark 9:23 - *"If you can?" said Jesus. "Everything is possible for one who believes."*

Cycle Breaking

Some are plagued by what seems to be inevitable generational cycles in their lives. For some, it's a cycle and lifestyle of being abused or being the abuser. For others, it's sickness, procrastination, poverty, divorce, unemployment, homosexuality, violence or premature death. For others still, it could be addiction. A prescription turned into a habit, a drink turned into a smoke, a smoke turned into a sniff and a sniff into shooting up drugs, and now you're caught up in a vicious cycle that is destroying your life and the lives of those around you.

The enemy loves addiction because it's mind altering. Once a mind is gone, the body and actions will follow. Before you know it, the enemy is using you as a puppet to manifest his destructive plots. It all shakes and breaks today! Reject and command every dysfunctional cycle that seems to be spinning your way to stop. There is power in the name of Jesus, so use it! Nothing you've done so far has worked, so try the real Answer today.

Let's ask God to deliver every cycle-bound person today. Let's ask Him to heal, deliver and set free. Let's ask Him to help our unbelief in any area because faith is the vehicle of God's miracles.

Psalm 50:15 - *Call on me in the day of trouble;*
I will deliver you, and you will honor me.

Psalm 107:6 - *"Lord, help!" they cried in their trouble,*
and He rescued them from their distress. (NLT)

Let's Examine Ourselves

Some have been praying for years for a change in a relationship, finances, health or for spiritual growth. Some seem to endure cycles of abuse, financial struggles and sickness. Some wonder why they always seem to be overlooked and ignored when it comes to big blessings and supernatural turnarounds. Sometimes it's a season of patience, and sometimes there is something hindering us from moving past a stagnate state.

It's time to purge our minds, emotions and spirits. It's time to release our stinking thinking, secret dark thoughts, hidden words, hidden agendas and the known and unknown sides of us that need to be healed and delivered. It's time for a spiritual X-ray and MRI.

Many things we won't outwardly admit. Very few admit when they are racist, jealous or manipulative, but the evidence is in their actions, motives and words. What are our deepest motives? Let's purge out the old today so we can receive the new.

Let's ask God for a supernatural cleansing and renewal. Let's ask Him to remove anything and anyone that is a distraction to our purpose in Him and a hindrance to the fullness of His power in our lives. Let's decrease in self so we can increase in Him.

Psalm 51:10-12 - *Create in me a pure heart, O God,*
   and renew a steadfast spirit within me.
Do not cast me from your presence
   or take your Holy Spirit from me.
Restore to me the joy of your salvation
   and grant me a willing spirit, to sustain me.

1 Corinthians 2:11-12 - *For who knows a person's thoughts except their own spirit within them? In the same way no one knows the thoughts of God except the Spirit of God. What we have received is not the spirit of the world, but the Spirit who is from God, so that we may understand what God has freely given us.*

Slow Your Roll

Have you checked on your loved ones today? Are you giving God, your spouse, children, relationships and/or friends fulfilling quality time? Do you really give a listening ear when being talked to? Or are your thoughts racing too fast to chase the next task at hand? Are you too occupied with work, ministry, wealth and the next business deal to take time to slow down and do something loving and spontaneous for the ones you care for?

God does not intend for us to be a people of imbalance. He is a God of balance and divine order. If we serve Him and yet our own lives, homes and relationships are a wreck, something is wrong. It's not always an attack of the enemy. Sometimes it's just us doing too much. God is the One who is omnipresent, so He doesn't need us to be all over the place.

It's a fast-paced world, and before we know it, a week, a month and another year have passed. When we reflect on the days as they flee, what have we gained? Is our family time balanced?

Let's ask God to lead us in obedience as He orders our steps to His peaceful and divine order. Sometimes less is more.

Psalm 90:17 - *And let the beauty of the Lord our God be upon us,*
  And establish the work of our hands for us;
  Yes, establish the work of our hands. (NKJV)

1 Corinthians 14:40 - *But everything should be done in a fitting and orderly way.*

Fight with the Right Weapons

Today is the day you must stop *talking* about change and start *being* about change! Today declare over your life that you will make spiritual history. Begin by identifying every area of your life that you have allowed to come full circle year after year, relationship after relationship, marriage after marriage and misery after misery.

What has you pressed down, broken and confused as abundant life passes you by? Call it out today, give it a name, and then change the name to what you want it to become. If it's Depression, change its name to Joy Unspeakable! If it's Confusion and Chaos, name it Peace That Surpasses All Understanding. Watch God change your present into a prophetic future of victory. We serve a God who gives us the supernatural ability to call those things that are not as though they already are! Operate in His free liberating power.

Let's ask God to break every cycle, every chain of bondage and every self-destructive issue of life that tries to keep us oppressed and distracted. Your race is already won. All you have to do is run it.

1 Corinthians 9:24 - *Don't you realize that in a race everyone runs, but only one person gets the prize? So run to win!* (NLT)

Seek God and Gain All

Living in a material world with material values can be challenging. We are subliminally programed to put our trust in things rather than in God. The world's system bombards us with various distractions. Some people become one-track minded on debt, houses, cars, top-of-the-line clothes, trips and job status. If we would just take a time-out from day-to-day thinking and ask God to lead us in His order of values, we will see the bigger picture.

Money can buy almost anything. It can buy sex, but it cannot buy love. It can buy health insurance, but it can't buy healing. It can buy beautiful houses, but it can't make your house a home. It can pay to send you anywhere in the world, but it can't buy you a ticket to Heaven. It can buy knowledge, but it can't buy wisdom. It can buy drugs to send you temporarily high above your problems, but it can't buy you peace which surpasses all understanding.

If we are out of sync with our priorities in life, let's ask God to keep us grounded in Him. Nothing tangible can buy the intangible. Seek God and gain it all.

Matthew 6:31-33 - *"So don't worry about these things, saying, 'What will we eat? What will we drink? What will we wear?' These things dominate the thoughts of unbelievers, but your heavenly Father already knows all your needs. Seek the Kingdom of God above all else, and live righteously, and he will give you everything you need."* (NLT)

The Motive Behind the Motion

As we seek the fullness of God's power in our lives so that we can impact the world around us, we must make sure we are transparent and do a daily self-check. God is not moved by our actions; He is moved by our motives. No matter how much sowing, preaching, ministering or encouraging we do, God knows the motive behind our every thought and action.

If we are not pleased by what we see within ourselves, we must ask God to do a spiritual, emotional and mental purge of our thoughts, motives and actions. He does not want us to worship Him in spirit and flattery, spirit and arrogance, spirit and selfishness, spirit and greed, spirit and hypocrisy, spirit and anger or spirit and unforgiveness; He wants a spirit of TRUTH. As we truly grow in Him, we minimize in self. This is when we see His increase in every area of our lives.

Let's ask God to help us to truly see ourselves for who we are. Let's ask Him to heal our broken areas and lead us into being the best in Him we can be. Let's talk less and listen more and ask God to help us be less so that we can be more.

Isaiah 29:13-14 - *And so the L<small>ORD</small> says,*
  "These people say they are mine.
 They honor me with their lips,
  but their hearts are far from me.
 And their worship of me
  is nothing but man-made rules learned by rote.

> *Because of this, I will once again astound these hypocrites*
> *with amazing wonders.*
> *The wisdom of the wise will pass away,*
> *and the intelligence of the intelligent will disappear."* (NLT)

John 4:24 - *"For God is Spirit, so those who worship him must worship in spirit and in truth."* (NLT)

Destiny Blockers

Refuse to be the blocker of your own destiny and purpose. In blocking yourself, you block others. Our existence is greater than us. We are created to add to the lives of others in one way or another.

We can choose to be vessels of good or evil. We can be builders or crushers, lifters of souls or destroyers. We can make life-long impacts for good or for bad. We can use our positions of authority to strengthen others or to weaken them. We can be spiritual, mental and emotional bullies or protectors. We can be sheep dogs or wolves.

What do you use your influence for? How do you want to be influenced? God did not create us as cookie-cutter clones. We are all created unique with different personalities. In all our uniqueness, love is the common ground because God is our Common Ground. He is Love. Our differences allow our strengths and weaknesses to complement each other so we can be edifiers of one another.

In all that we do toward others, let's ask God to guide us through His love. How do you want to be taught, led, reproved, instructed or corrected? In all our opportunities of influence, let's ask God to lead us in love as we lead others. Anything done without love is empty.

Romans 14:19 - *Therefore let us pursue the things which make for peace and the things by which one may edify another.* (NKJV)

1 Thessalonians 5:11 - *So encourage each other and build each other up, just as you are already doing.* (NLT)

God Spoke and Created, Therefore Speak and Create

The atmosphere is fertile for your breakthrough! The air we breathe has transferring power! Speak into your atmosphere today! With every breath, declare, decree and prophesy over yourself VICTORY!

Look at your bills, debts, and seemingly-impossible situations and declare God's vindicating, restoring, reviving, healing, prospering and debt-cancelling power. This Earth is God's and ALL that is in it, so whatever we need, God already has it! If it is your job situation, walk around your building, office, cubicle or desk and speak wisdom, promotion, professional restoration and positional alignment! If it's family issues, speak unity, peace, discipline and respect! If it's a ministry, speak salvation, harvest, healing, deliverance, laborers, power, revelation and obedience. If it is an unjust situation, speak boldness, fairness, favor, order and vindication. Whenever the enemy tries to enter your camp, guard your gates today through the power of faith-filled, radical, bold and fervent prayer. Victory is yours for the taking.

Let's ask God to lead us in being better spiritual, emotional and financial stewards. Let's ask Him to impart His power in all that concerns us. As we ask, let us believe. As we believe, we shall receive. God spoke and created. Therefore speak and create.

Hebrews 11:3 - *By faith we understand that the entire universe was formed at God's command, that what we now see did not come from anything that can be seen.(NLT)*

Meek Is Not Weak

As we grow in God and try to live according to our purpose in Him, we often have to shed old behaviors. Some of us may have had bad tempers, sharp and perverse tongues, or maybe someone had a very impatient spirit. Sometimes, during our seasons of transformation, we may encounter character tests. Situations will arise that may tempt you to go back to your old ways, old reactions or explosive tempers. You may get an immediate emotional satisfaction, but it will leave you spiritually convicted and socially judged.

The enemy loves to kill our witness by drawing us backward rather than forward. Do not let the dysfunctions and issues of others become your reality. Do not give your power away to an emotional fling. We are to rise above the clouds of contention. Do not allow evil to break your wings. You are striving toward your next level in God. Resistance makes your stronger, so do not give in.

Let's ask God to strengthen us during our tests and trials. Let's ask Him to harness our flesh and strengthen our spirit. Let's pray for the wisdom to be the example He calls us to be ... even when we don't know how. Being meek does not make you weak. You are mighty in Him.

Proverbs 16:32 - *He who is slow to anger is better than the mighty, And he who rules his spirit than he who captures a city.* (NASB)

Every Season Is Your Season

Even though we encounter various seasons in life, every season is your season. It may not be your season of harvest, but it is a season of purpose. Before your seasons of harvest comes, the other seasons are for preparation. We can't just stand idly and expect to sing *It's a New Season* without preparing for it.

Whether it is harvest time or dry times, each season requires us to first sow faith. You must first believe your harvest is coming. You must first believe God is able to provide, heal, deliver and prosper you. You must first believe He is a Life-Changer. Each season is a preparatory time, to pray, believe, be obedient, work, toil, plant, prepare and patiently wait in faith.

You will reap all that you have sown at the appointed time. Do not be discouraged if you are not presently seeing the fruits of your labor. They are on the way.

> Let's ask God to encourage our spirits as we await the great. Let's ask Him to lead us in being patient and diligent as we sow faith in every season of life. Let's ask Him to lead us as we seek His will in all that concerns us.

Romans 12:12 - *Rejoicing in hope, patient in tribulation, continuing steadfastly in prayer.* (ASV)

Galatians 6:9 - *And let us not grow weary while doing good, for in due season we shall reap if we do not lose heart.* (NKJV)

Spiritual Cancer

Spiritual complacency is like spiritual cancer; it slowly eats away at your healthy spiritual cells of zeal, faith, vision, gifting, revelation and prayer. When this cancer sets in, you grow spiritually lethargic and no longer want to pray, study, believe or walk in eager boldness to live out your purpose in God.

When we constantly consume the spiritual cancer-causing agents of compromise, settling, arrogance, pride, slothfulness and inferiority, we begin to spiritually weaken. You are called for such a time as this, to be who you were created to be. No one can do what you can do in the way God created you to do it. Stop looking around at others, and start looking in the mirror and beholding your greatness. You were created in His image to do greater works through Him.

Let's ask God to heal us from every spiritual hindrance that tries to block our purpose in Him. God didn't give us life to die with our purpose and unused gifts. Live on purpose.

John 14:12 - *"I tell you the truth, anyone who believes in me will do the same works I have done, and even greater works, because I am going to be with the Father." (NLT)*

Hebrews 6:11-12 - *And we desire that each one of you show the same diligence to the full assurance of hope until the end, that you do not become sluggish, but imitate those who through faith and patience inherit the promises. (NKJV)*

Loved to Love

This world is filled with haters of happiness. The enemy and his vessels do not want you joyful, happy, prosperous, healthy or successful on any natural or spiritual front. However, haters of happiness have no more power than they are mentally allowed to have.

Some just do not like to see others happy, due to their own miseries of life. Some resent the fact that others have joy unspeakable and peace that surpasses all understanding. Many times they are unhappy and resentful due to the fact that life just seems to have dealt them an unfortunate hand. All that could go wrong always does, and the breaks others get seem far from their world. However, as lights in a dark world, we must realize that shunning the depressed, downtrodden and miserable is not the answer. God's love covers a multitude of sins, miseries, bad breaks, misfortunes, injustices, bad outcomes, bad attitudes and sick mindsets.

Love is the vehicle of world-changing power. Only love can conquer all. God IS love, so what HE IS is the answer. His love covered our multitude of imperfections, and what He does for one He is able to do for all.

Let's ask God to teach us how to love. Let's ask Him to lift up the unloved, misunderstood and broken. Broken people break others. God's love picks up the pieces and makes us whole.

Proverbs 10:12 - *Hatred stirs up strife,*
But love covers all sins. (NKJV)

Colossians 3:12-14 - *Since God chose you to be the holy people he loves, you must clothe yourselves with tenderhearted mercy, kindness,* *humility, gentleness, and patience. Make allowance for each other's faults, and forgive anyone who offends you. Remember, the Lord forgave you, so you must forgive others. Above all, clothe yourselves with love, which binds us all together in perfect harmony.* (NLT)

Stay Connected to Your High Tower

We can often get discouraged when bad decisions and choices seem to have destroyed the possibilities of another chance at a better life. Maybe poor choices in relationships or marriages seem to have set your life back. Maybe you were not the best example while rearing children, and you feel your past mistakes contribute to their present issues. Maybe you feel you missed a call to ministry because you have a past that haunts you. Be encouraged. Just because a plane may fly off course does not mean it will not land at its destination. A detour and re-route is not a crash and burn.

Sometimes your past imperfections are a ministry in themselves. We often lead others out of the issues we have been through. Misery and mistakes are often the birthing grounds for ministry and teaching. You have boldness when you speak on those things that are a part of you. What often brought you pain brings you passion.

Let's ask God to reroute our minds as He reroutes our journey. Let's ask Him to mend every broken place created by our mistakes. Let's ask Him to give us a spirit of obedience as He guides our steps to new levels in Him. And, if we fly off course, let's make sure we stay connected to our High Tower. There is no mistake in Him.

Proverbs 3:6-8 - *In all your ways acknowledge Him,*
   And He shall direct your paths.
   Do not be wise in your own eyes;
   Fear the Lord *and depart from evil.*

> *It will be health to your flesh,*
> *And strength to your bones.* (NKJV)

Proverbs 16:9 - *A man's heart plans his way,*
*But the L*ORD *directs his steps.* (NKJV)

The Pit of Spiritual Pornography

It can be discouraging to live in a world where favoritism often seems to override favor, where lust is overshadowing love, where pornographic movements are tickling flesh rather than hearts, where perversion is stealing the media, movie and music spotlights, and where the rich get richer while the less fortunate are usually the most giving and generous.

Be encouraged. We still win. This is why we must walk by faith and not by sight. This is why we are taught that faith without works is dead. In our world, God has placed people in every area to be an impact for reviving change and to speak out and up against the wiles of evil. The Lord our God is asking: What are we doing with our positions of influence? What stand are you taking? What change are you making? What standards are you pulling down or setting up that will shake an evil influence out of its place? What are you doing to stop perversion, disrespect and injustice from prevailing? We are not called to be prostituted and pimped for evil to sell.

Let's ask God to give us a supernatural boldness to stand and speak for His righteousness, fairness, justice, compassion, reproof and truth. Let's pull down every stronghold of fear and compromise. What have we done that set others back rather than forward? We are accountable for we do AND fail to do.

James 2:2-4, 14-17 and 26 - *For example, suppose someone comes into your meeting dressed in fancy clothes and expensive jewelry, and another comes in who is poor and dressed in dirty clothes. If you give special attention and a good seat to the rich person, but* *you say to the poor one, "You can stand over there, or else sit on the floor" — well, doesn't this discrimination show that your judgments are guided by evil motives? ... What good is it, dear brothers and sisters, if you say you have faith but don't show it by your actions? Can that kind of faith save anyone? Suppose you see a brother or sister who has no food or clothing, and you say, "Good-bye and have a good day; stay warm and eat well" — but then you don't give that person any food or clothing. What good does that do? So you see, faith by itself isn't enough. Unless it produces good deeds, it is dead and useless. ... Just as the body is dead without breath, so also faith is dead without good works.* (NLT)

Don't Be a Spiritual Selfie

There are many people sitting on dead gifts, dead ministries, dead words and dead opportunities because they are more focused on being in the forefront, rather than being content with the background. Some of the greatest works are seen before the worker is seen. If we are ruled by the acknowledgement and elevation of man, the enemy will have a field day blocking our greatness in God. If he knows you have to be publicly acknowledged before you move in your gifts, you will remain hidden in dormancy.

Let's ask ourselves: Are we okay with others being praised? Are we okay if we are not in the limelight? Can we still do our best and give our best when the microphone is not in our hand and the pats on the back are few? If you are a pastor, are you offended when others use some of your words to set captives free? What's more important, the souls being saved or your acknowledgement?

Let's pray to stay God-focused and not self-focused. For some, life is one big selfie. Let's ask God to help us decrease in the pride of flesh so we can increase in Him. We come alive when we die to flesh.

Romans 12:3 - *Because of the privilege and authority God has given me, I give each of you this warning: Don't think you are better than you really are. Be honest in your evaluation of yourselves, measuring yourselves by the faith God has given us.* (NLT)

Trusting Him

Your back is against the wall. You have tried for the loan. You have contemplated the bankruptcy. You are wondering what you can sell. The doctor said the medicine is not working, so now you have to increase the dosage. The job didn't come through or the one that did is not the environment you thought it was. What do you do? You thank God because you are in one of the best spiritual places you can ever imagine. You are at the place where you bring God in remembrance of His promises and remind Him that He said He was your Provider, Healer, Deliver, and Defense.

Thank God for not being a man that He would lie, but thank Him for being the God of everlasting truth. He's the Promise-Keeper, Way-Maker, Miracle-Worker and Testimony Creator. You are in the place where faith manifests the things that seem impossible in your life. You are about to see God operate as He did when He created all things. He spoke and made everything manifest out of nothing, and He can do that for you too. He is going to multiply your lack and go beyond the doctor's report. He's going to use you to change your environment.

Let's ask God to remove our fear and increase our faith when we face what seems impossible. Nothing is impossible unless you let it be.

Jeremiah 32:17 - *"O Sovereign Lord! You made the heavens and earth by your strong hand and powerful arm. Nothing is too hard for you!"* (NLT)

Know His Voice and a Stranger You Will Not Follow

With it being very evident that we are on the brink of a spiritual awakening, we must realize that end-time signs require end-time faith. We must make sure we are sober and vigilant during these times of spiritual confusion. We must make sure we are intimately connected with God so we can clearly hear and understand His voice among the many distracting voices of our world.

There are voices of unbelief, logic, new-age religion, demonic influence, self-glorification, false doctrine and those who will rise with eloquent words and wonderful works who will do nothing but tickle your emotions and ears, leaving you spiritually lost, unchanged and confused. God's voice is sound and clear, and when you learn His voice you will never follow the voice of the strange ones. If you have been confused today or do not know what you believe, ask God to reveal Himself to you. He will.

Let's ask God to direct our paths, lead our spirits and draw closer to us, as we draw closer to Him. Let's ask Him to manifest Himself in every area of our lives and mold us according to His will, as we pursue our progressive purpose in Him.

John 10:27 - *My sheep listen to my voice; I know them, and they follow me.* (NLT)

1 Timothy 4:1 - *Now the Holy Spirit tells us clearly that in the last times some will turn away from the true faith; they will follow deceptive spirits and teachings that come from demons.* (NLT)

Don't Give Your Power Away

What are you giving your power to? What have you allowed to control your mind, spirit and actions? Is it an ongoing feud between a spouse, family members or friends that you have allowed to cause you to lower your standards of integrity and character? Is the pride of others causing to become stubborn, prideful and unforgiving? Is it a bad habit, addiction or a naysayer?

Are you captive to your own weaknesses and keep giving them power by not trying to strengthen yourself in the areas of temperance, patience and spiritual obedience? Do you allow the actions of others to control yours? Or is it money, a new home, a new car, a flourishing business or ministry that has caused you to lose sight of where your seasons of success and blessings really come from? Whatever it is that you give power and attention to more than God is an idol. Whatever causes you to be less than what God created you to be is not in your best interests. Whatever causes your standards to drop in all areas of your life is slowly trying to minimize your greatness in order to prop itself up on your strengths.

Let's ask God to realign our minds, hearts and spirits with His will and purpose in us. Let's ask Him to expose and strengthen our areas of weakness through His revelatory power.

Exodus 20:3 - *"You must not have any other god but me."* (NLT)

1 Corinthians 10:13 - *The temptations in your life are no different from what others experience. And God is faithful. He will not allow the temptation to be more than you can stand. When you are tempted, he will show you a way out so that you can endure.* (NLT)

Breaking the Cycle of Abuse

There is so much abuse in the world, and we usually only see what is reported or witnessed. A life of abuse is tormenting mentally, physically, emotionally and spiritually. There are those who cannot be themselves because they are forced to live in a personal prison. Slowly but surely they are often isolated from family, friends, church relationships and other networks of social, emotional and spiritual peace. Anything that appears to give the abused strength is brutalized out of them one tactic at a time. Abusive words escalate to abusive actions. A word becomes a grab, a push becomes a slap, a slap becomes a punch, then a kick, bat, bullet or knife.

The abused are often under surveillance, stalked and terrorized while hiding behind a veil of confidence, smiles and falsified boldness. The cycles of highs and lows, good times and bad, often leave the abused confused and further disappointed, as they give the abuser chance after chance for hopeful change. Know this: God is your Refuge, Rock and Defense. If this is you, you are not hopeless and helpless. God does not will for anyone to be abused. Abuse is not love, and excuses are dangerous enablers.

Let's pray for every man, woman, and child enduring verbal, emotional and physical abuse. Let's ask God to also heal the abusers and mend the root of their pain. Hurting people hurt others. God is an edifier, not a wrecking ball of pain and negativity. Let's ask God to lead the abused to refuge and resources that will bring new life, not death.

Psalm 10:17-18 - L*ord*, *you know the hopes of the helpless. Surely you will hear their cries and comfort them. You will bring justice to the orphans and the oppressed, so mere people can no longer terrify them.* (NLT)

Psalm 147:3 - *He heals the brokenhearted and binds up their wounds.*

Psalm 107:20 - *He sent His word and healed them, And delivered them from their destructions.* (NKJV)

Masks of Religiosity

Halloween is a day that, in many parts of the world, children innocently see as a time to dress up, put on make-up and become that super hero they admire or some monster, and then eat candy until they drop. Many Christians deem this to be a wicked day, a day of witches and demonic activity. And, yes, some have taken it to another level, as with all things.

However, let's flip the perspective. How many masks of religion are worn every day by Christians? How many forms of godliness do we see every day that mask who we are really called to be? The enemy is pressing in to make the Church a goblin of religion. Tricks with no treats? Halloween is every day in this dark world, and the biggest horror story of all time is having a light to shine and keeping the power turned off during the darkest hours.

The enemy tries to come in our camp every day, so let's shine on him. Let's take off the masks of religion and judgment and give someone around us a piece of God today.

Isaiah 42:16 – *I will lead the blind by ways they have not known, along unfamiliar paths I will guide them; I will turn the darkness into light before them and make the rough places smooth. These are the things I will do; I will not forsake them.*

Stay in Your Lane

Each of us has a purpose to do something great for God, and God works on each of us at various interlinking intervals because our lives are not our own. We are accountable for our words, actions and deeds because they impact others spiritually, emotionally, mentally and physically. Once we get the revelation that our choices, actions and words make impacts on others beyond our understanding, we will be more diligent in our pursuit of spiritual progress.

Life's circumstances can be consuming and distracting. God is pruning you for your Great. Do not try to keep up with the growth patterns of others. Fast starts do not guarantee strong finishes. Sometimes we have to step back before stepping up, sit before standing, walk before running and fall before rising.

Let's ask God to give us divine confidence as we run the race set before us.

Proverbs 9:9 - *Instruct the wise,*
and they will be even wiser.
Teach the righteous,
and they will learn even more. (NLT)

Hebrews 12:1 - *Therefore we also, since we are surrounded by so great a cloud of witnesses, let us lay aside every weight, and the sin which so easily ensnares us, and let us run with endurance the race that is set before us.* (NKJV)

Lay Aside Your Weight

God's Spirit is liberating. There is no bondage in Him. When you feel pressed, confused and overwhelmed with the cares of life and do not see any light at the end of your tunnel, release yourself to God. We are usually weighed down when we try to carry our burdens alone.

We were not created to carry burdens. God is our Burden Bearer and Caretaker. He's our Defense, Counselor, Provider and Healer. In all that we worry about, He is the Answer and Pathfinder. He is the One who leads us through every trial, and He is the One who gives us the power to win every battle. When we lean to our own limited understanding and rely on our own limited resources, we feel oppressed. Give God your highest praise through the press, and worship past the worry.

Let's ask God to lead us, as we lay aside every weight that tries to blind our liberation in Him. Our God is Supernatural. Tap into your new level in Him, and watch your weights drop off.

Galatians 5:1 - *Stand fast therefore in the liberty by which Christ has made us free, and do not be entangled again with a yoke of bondage.* (NKJV)

Relationship vs. Religion

Religion has caused many to fall away from seeking an intimate relationship with God. Those who do not know God personally have allowed man to make God seem like a rigid rule-maker with no compassion and no desire for relationship. Religion has made God appear as a controlling superior who has a list of requirements with no guidance on how to live His plan for our lives.

Know this: God is a loving God who will never ask any more of us than He is willing to give us the power to achieve. He is more fair, more loving, more patient, more compassionate, more merciful and more holy than we could ever be. Do not be discouraged during your progressive walk to personal excellence. Though man may slay us during our journey, God is there to pick up the pieces and put us back together again for the next round. He never gives up on us, so don't give up on Him or yourself.

Let's ask God to remove the fear of accountability. Let's ask Him to heal those who have been beaten down during their valley experiences. Let's ask Him to reveal Himself to all who seek a true and intimate relationship with Him. His arms are wider than our imperfections.

Jeremiah 17:10 - *"But I, the LORD, search all hearts
   and examine secret motives.
 I give all people their due rewards,
   according to what their actions deserve."* (NLT)

Romans 14:12 - *Yes, each of us will give a personal account to God.* (NLT)

1 Thessalonians 5:11 - *So encourage each other and build each other up, just as you are already doing.* (NLT)

Press to Progress

There are times when we need to give ourselves constructive criticism. We all need it. If we constantly drink from the waters of compliments, fanfare and flattery, we will always be thirsty for truth. Flattery is mere chatter, while truth has sound substance. Truth will always bear witness with us, whether we embrace it or not.

When we only stay in the comfort zones of complacency and established victory, we never go further. There is no progress in familiarity. When we become too familiar with ourselves and others, we may close our ears and minds to fertile opportunities for growth. When we find ourselves in a non-progressive state spiritually, socially, professionally or emotionally, we must truthfully ask ourselves: Why are we here? The truth is there, if only we would face it.

Maybe we are still stagnant due to slothfulness, lack of drive, fear or self-doubt. Maybe we draw and are drawn to purpose distractors. Maybe some only like to lead, so they cannot comfortably follow. Maybe we are focusing so much on where someone else is that we can't get to where we are supposed to be going.

Let's ask God to shake us all out of the trap of stagnation through His infinite wisdom. Let's ask Him to give us a spirit of obedience and wisdom, as we pursue the path to our manifested purpose in Him. Let's pray for more faith and zeal, as we press forward to personal excellence in Him.

Proverbs 12:15 - *The way of a fool is right in his own eyes, But he who heeds counsel is wise.* (NKJV)

Proverbs 19:20 - *Listen to counsel and receive instruction, That you may be wise in your latter days.* (NKJV)

Conquer Your Mountain Before It Conquers You

Conquer your mountain or it will conquer you. When facing obstacles in life, the circumstantial mountains can seem impossible to climb. It's not always just the mountain; it's the terrain that comes with it (such as the thorns of rejection, the ground holes of depression, the brier bushes of betrayal and the rocks of hardened hearts).

No matter what mountain you are facing, you were created to be a mountain climber, overcomer, thorn puller and valley survivor. Your mountain is just another opportunity for God to show Himself strong and mighty.

As you climb, God is moving. As you rise above your naysayers, your enemies, your lack, your emotional tragedies and your I-can'ts and I-wont's, YOU WILL, YOU SHALL and YOU MUST.

> Let's ask God to move our mountains as we climb in His power. Let's ask Him to show us the lesson in all of our mountainous terrains, valley experiences, dark hours and winters. He is a Season Changer and Mountain Mover. All you have to do is speak, pray, believe, walk and watch. Don't let your mountain move you. MOVE YOUR MOUNTAIN through HIM.

Psalm 18:33 - *He makes my feet like the feet of deer,*
And sets me on my high places. (NKJV)

Speaking to Your Void

Over the course of our lives, many of us have been told at least once to be quiet. Whether it was because we were talking too much, out of turn or out of order, we have been told to hush. It's important because even in our natural world our words matter.

Our words can be used to build up or tear down. The wrong words can confuse others, leading them to a place of emotional destruction or mental anguish. Our words have the ability to mold lives. Whether it be a child, adult, acquaintance, friend or a congregation, our words have accountability, life and power. After all, before God did anything else, HE SPOKE to voids. All was void until God SPOKE.

The enemy knows the power of our words, so he tries to shut the mouths of faith. Through trials, tribulations and exhausting hills and valleys of circumstances, he tries to silence the power of God's Holy Spirit that lives on the inside of you. No matter how down, defeated, tired, frustrated or lost you may feel, SPEAK to your void. Whatever it is, speak forth what you want it to be, according to God's Word.

Let's ask God to give us all the boldness to speak past our circumstances. Let's ask Him to guide us through His Word, as we seek His answers for our lives. He is the Way, the Truth and the Life. That's a clear path, so let's seek it and speak it. Seek His Way, live in His Truth, and live the Life He's promised you.

Genesis 1:1-4 - *In the beginning God created the heavens and the earth. The earth was formless and empty, and darkness covered the deep waters. And the Spirit of God was hovering over the surface of the waters.*

Then God said, "Let there be light," and there was light. And God saw that the light was good. Then he separated the light from the darkness. (NLT)

Mark 11:23 - *"I tell you the truth, you can say to this mountain, 'May you be lifted up and thrown into the sea,' and it will happen. But you must really believe it will happen and have no doubt in your heart."* (NLT)

The Seasonal Pain of Parenting

When you are a parent or guardian, the strain of rearing children can transcend all aspects of your life. When your children go through seasons of rebellion, negative influence, peer pressure and bad choices, these dark times can cause you to feel like an outcast. Their doings may strain your friendships, marriages and other long established relationships. Many times parents are treated as their children's bad choices, judged as if it's something they have done wrong. No matter how much you try, pray and reach out for the support of others, you may feel shunned due to the fact that no one wants to be affected by your dark season and the demonic activity that is attacking your children.

Everyone has a right to protect their own, and when yours is a social threat, it can be painful, embarrassing and lonely sometimes. KNOW THIS: God is still God, and HE is a Healer, Deliverer, Vindicator, Refuge and ROCK. When you are rooted in Him, your children are covered. Although they may seem to stray, they WILL return to the way of power and righteousness. They will be redirected and re-established. Be encouraged. Your misery will become a ministry to others who will endure the very test that you and yours are now passing. Your children will RISE.

Let's pray for parents and families who are going through challenging times with their children. Let's ask God to break every yoke and pull down every stronghold. Hold your head up and face your fight because God never loses a battle. He says train them up in the way they should go, and when they are OLDER they will not

depart from it. When they are younger they may. Therefore sow now and reap later.

Proverbs 22:6 - *Direct your children onto the right path,*
  and when they are older,
  they will not leave it. (NLT)

Romans 12:12 - *Rejoice in our confident hope. Be patient in trouble,*
  and keep on praying. (NLT)

Speak the Answer, Not the Problem

No matter what you are facing, God is bigger than that! For everything you are enduring, God has an answer for it. His answers may not always be pleasing to our impatience, but they are always best. God's answers will grow us, edify us to new levels in Him, reprove us, correct us and guide us.

If you are facing financial bondage, God's answer is the whole Earth is His and the fullness of it. Anything we lack or need, He IS the Provision, Surplus and Increase, and He is able and willing to bring forth our abundance. If's it's failing relationships, family chaos, national turmoil or rebellious children, His answer is He is the one who has the heart of kings in the palm of His hand, so surely He has your wife's heart, your husband's heart, your loved one's heart, your children's heart, and our national leader's heart in His Hand and can turn them in the direction they need to be in through Him, not us. If it's sickness, disease or a death report, His answer is He is our Healer and we shall live and not die.

Let's pray for a revelation on the limitless power of God. Let's pray to never hold Him to our limited standards and imperfect ways. Even on our best days, we will NEVER be Him. Trust Him today, and stop saying what your problem says. Instead, speak what HE says.

Proverbs 21:1-2 - *The king's heart is like a stream of water directed by the LORD;*
he guides it wherever he pleases.

> *People may be right in their own eyes,*
> *but the* L<small>ORD</small> *examines their heart.* (NLT)

Matthew 7:11 - *So if you sinful people know how to give good gifts to your children, how much more will your heavenly Father give good gifts to those who ask him.* (NLT)

The After-Effects of Grief

Today we will pray for the grieving. When tragedy, sickness and disease take the lives of loved ones, the grief often runs well beyond the death. Everyone grieves differently, and there is no set deadline for when grief and mourning should cease. During these dreadful dark days, the enemy will use grief as an avenue to bring family division, marital stress, seclusion and reclusion, silence and emotional numbness to compound the sadness.

Death and grief often bring divorce, anger and depression to the loved ones left to bear their loss. It's a domino effect of demise, and some are left feeling hopeless, helpless, broken and alone. The joy of the Lord is our strength, so the enemy will go to all lengths to sabotage that strength. Be encouraged today. God is the Repairer of Broken Places, the Strength of our lives, and His peace surpasses all understanding. He restores joy, renews strength, renews minds and comforts us in seemingly comfortless places.

Let's pray for those enduring grief and its secondary effects. Let's ask God to mend every broken heart and rejuvenate every broken spirit. He turns darkness into light and sadness to joy. He's the Light of the World. Let's ask Him to shine in every dark hour.

Psalm 34:18 - *The Lord is close to the brokenhearted; he rescues those whose spirits are crushed.* (NLT)

Psalm 112:7 - *They do not fear bad news; they confidently trust the Lord to care for them.* (NLT)

Matthew 5:4 - *God blesses those who mourn, for they will be comforted.* (NLT)

The Church Needs Prayer

With so many churches coming up in many communities, you would think we would see more of the manifestation of God's power in our lives, communities, leadership and nation. There is a form of godliness that brings no power, and until we worship and operate in Spirit and in Truth, the cup will remain half-full. End-time issues require end-time faith and power. The fullness of God brings salvation, healing, miracles, deliverance, wisdom, restoration, love, unity and peace.

Going from Sunday best to Monday through Saturday worst is not going to move God or the mountains of our circumstances. The most dangerous spiritual threat is a church led by flesh, religion and tradition, and not the anointing. Flesh never broke a yoke. Tradition causes churches to hinder rather than release. Tradition says a woman should not speak, teach or preach when that could be the vessel God chooses to use to set a captive free. If God says He will use a rock to praise Him if we won't, surely He can use a woman or any other vessel He chooses. When a church program breaks the flow of God's Spirit, it's time to check it. It's not about us; it's about souls. We are all called to decrease and let God increase.

Let's ask God to give pastors, ministers and leaders a revelation of His will as they lead. Let's pray that God will give churches a new revelation of order that will usher Him in through a flow of worship, praise and His living revelatory Word. We need to be fed by the Spirit before knowing when the next church dinner is. Let's die to flesh so we can live in Him.

Luke 19:37-40 - *Then, as He was now drawing near the descent of the Mount of Olives, the whole multitude of the disciples began to rejoice and praise God with a loud voice for all the mighty works they had seen, saying:*

"'Blessed is the King who comes in the name of the Lord!' Peace in heaven and glory in the highest!"

And some of the Pharisees called to Him from the crowd, "Teacher, rebuke Your disciples."
But He answered and said to them, "I tell you that if these should keep silent, the stones would immediately cry out." (NKJV)

Being Prayerfully Proactive, Not Reactive

In today's world, we are seeing an increase of violence and religious uproar and turmoil on every front. What's amazing is this: in the aftermath of tragedies, news headlines often proclaim "A COMMUNITY PRAYS" or "A NATION PRAYS." But this should be every day, not just in the wake of tragedy or as a response to disaster. If we, as a people and a nation, would be more proactive in prayer instead of reactive, we would see mighty moves of God on the very fronts where disaster is trying to make its home.

God is a living God, a God of power, deliverance, protection, security, abundance, mercy, healing and grace. He does not will for us to endure such days of doom and tragedy but gives us a promise to never forsake us and to always be with us. We are the ones who have forsaken Him.

Let's give thanks to God for being who He is, and let's ask Him to forgive us for the many times we only come to Him when we need something. Let's pray for a spirit of proactive prayer, worship and praise in all situations and at all times because God is worthy of glory as the Ground Breaker, World Shaker and Stronghold Puller. He is still God, and He will never lose His power. Seek, pray, believe and receive, for He's available. Are we?

Deuteronomy 31:6 - *So be strong and courageous! Do not be afraid and do not panic before them. For the L*ORD *your God will personally go ahead of you. He will neither fail you nor abandon you.* (NLT)

Warfare Prayer

The power of prayer covering is a necessity in life. If Jesus prayed, then we know we definitely need to! With the days becoming more violent, vicious and hateful, we, as the believers, need to guard our gates.

The enemy guards his gates every day. He makes sure he keeps people lost and sick. He tries to shut the influential mouths of faith, focus and power by bombarding the life of God's children with confusion, perversion, family division, church collapse, fear and educational decay.

Satan is also pursuing generational spiritual genocide. He doesn't want the upcoming generations to have even a clue about the power of God within, so he distracts them with social sabotage and evil influence and tries to make evil look good, so the spiritual babies will believe a lie before God's divine truth.

Let's collectively take a conscious spiritual and prayerful stand and ask God to guard our families, churches, transportation, job, finances and friends. Let's ask Him to shut every door that has been opened to evil activity. Let's lift the lost.

Let's ask God to be our front and rear guard from every assignment of destruction on our lives. No weapon formed against you shall prosper. Speak it, believe it, and watch God defend, vindicate and shield you. As evil preys unceasingly upon us, we must PRAY unceasingly, fervently and faithfully.

Ephesians 6:12 - *For we are not fighting against flesh-and-blood enemies, but against evil rulers and authorities of the unseen world, against mighty powers in this dark world, and against evil spirits in the heavenly places.* (NLT)

Guard Your Gates

When it comes to identifying who and what we need in our lives, we must ask ourselves: do those things and people do what God does? Do the people, things, and places we expose ourselves to bring emotional, spiritual and physical life to us? Or do they kill, steal and destroy us? Do the things, places and people you draw to you or allow to be drawn to you bring you abundance, peace and joy? Or do they bring you stress, anxiety and confusion? Are you left lifted or oppressed? Do they feed you with the fruits of God's Spirit or poison your peace? Do the things you allow to enter your ears, eyes, body and spiritual gates leave you feeling fulfilled and satisfied or empty and sick in the mind, body and spirit?

In order to soar to the higher things of God, we must release the weights of oppression that try to break our wings. God's power destroys yokes, pulls down strongholds and brings us abundant life. If something or someone is not lining up with God's will for our life, then it's a derailed track leading to delayed growth and destiny distraction.

Let's ask God to align everything in our lives with His will. Let's ask Him to remove the distractions so we can live in His will and live out our purpose in Him.

John 10:10 - *"The thief's purpose is to steal and kill and destroy. My purpose is to give them a rich and satisfying life."* (NLT)

Galatians 5:22-23 - *But the Holy Spirit produces this kind of fruit in our lives: love, joy, peace, patience, kindness, goodness, faithfulness, gentleness, and self-control. There is no law against these things!* (NLT)

The Revelation of Rest

The revelation of rest is still at the forefront. God wants us to know that if we only realized how many car accidents, plane crashes, critically bad decisions, failing ministries, pre-mature deaths, failed classes, lost jobs, lost marriages, lost businesses, chronic illnesses and behavior disorders were due to lack of rest we would be astonished! There are so many misdiagnoses due to lack of sleep.

Today's busy schedules for children, as well as adults, is causing a chronic lack of rest. Pushing a mind and body excessively without rest leads to mental, spiritual and physical demise. Short tempers, addiction to sleeping meds, abuse, bad behavior, lack of quality time and romance is destroying healthy lives and relationships due to sleep lost.

Let's ask God to give us all a revelation on the rest He wills for us. Let's ask Him to individually touch every mind, body and spirit that is in desperate need of rest. Let's ask Him to rearrange every imbalanced schedule and bring rest, peace, healing and restoration.

Psalm 4:8 - *In peace I will lie down and sleep, for you alone, O Lord, will keep me safe.* (NLT)

Our ALL in ALL

Today we are going to get back to the basics. We, as a human race, have become so obsessed with science, technology and this new age of knowledge that it can almost seem like the creation is trying to make itself equal with God. How can a creation supersede its Creator or a pot make itself the Potter? God is the only Beginning and End and nothing in between that spectrum will be equal with Him.

There is no philosophy, logic, science, history lesson or discovery that will ever be beyond God. A molecule never saved a soul. A big bang never healed the sick or raised the dead. Philosophy can't explain God, and the miracle-working power of active faith makes logic mute. God is a living God, not a hypothesis.

Let's ask God to manifest His truth in every area of life today and always. Let's ask Him for a supernatural manifestation of His promises and power in our spirits, minds, emotions, bodies, finances and circumstances. He is our ALL in ALL. Give Him your ALL and ALL—mind, body and spirit, and behold the wonder of His everlasting works.

Isaiah 40:28 - *Have you never heard?*
  Have you never understood?
  The L*ord* *is the everlasting God,*
   the Creator of all the earth.
  He never grows weak or weary.
   No one can measure the depths of his understanding. (NLT)

God Is Bigger than Your Battle

What's your pattern? When trouble hits, do you fold in doubt or stand in faith? Do you waver at the sight of trouble or believe past the problem? God wants us to run to Him with immovable expectation and faith. He tells us to come to Him like children for a reason.

Have you ever noticed that when children are confronted with fearful situations, the first thing they do is say: I'm going to tell my momma (daddy, or some other guardian they have complete trust in)? They know, without a shadow of a doubt, they will be defended, shielded, protected and victoriously led. How much faster should we humbly and joyfully run to our ALL-POWERFUL God, who has never lost a battle, controls the world and all that dwells in it, and has whatever we need in overflowing abundance?

Let's ask God to renew our minds and stir up our faith. Let's ask Him to manifest Himself in the midst of our oppression. Your situation is only another opportunity for God to show Himself strong and mighty. He's our Faith-Shaker and Way-Maker. Be encouraged today because God is bigger than your battle.

Matthew 18:3 - *"Assuredly, I say to you, unless you are converted and become as little children, you will by no means enter the kingdom of heaven."* (NKJV)

Matthew 21:22 - *"And whatever things you ask in prayer, believing, you will receive."* (NKJV)

1 Corinthians 15:58 - *Therefore, my dear brothers and sisters, stand firm. Let nothing move you. Always give yourselves fully to the work of the Lord, because you know that your labor in the Lord is not in vain.* (NKJV)

Go Deeper

We are going to go deeper. No more scratching the spiritual surface. No more just enough. No more just wanting the ends to meet. No more just treating the symptoms. We are going to the root.

Whatever it is you are enduring has a root. Whether it's divorce, depression, confusion, bankruptcy, lost homes, lost jobs, lost children or lost relationships, there is a spiritual root to everything growing in your natural garden. God can and will heal your roots. There is no mediocrity in Him. Whatever you are facing, begin to pray big, think bigger and believe beyond the charade of limitation.

> **Let's ask God to lead us in removing our limits. Let's ask Him to help our unbelief when our issues seem bigger than our faith. Let's thank Him for His supernatural provision, healing and restoration. Dig in and watch what comes up.**

Jeremiah 17:7-8 - *But blessed is the one who trusts in the Lord,*
   whose confidence is in him.
They will be like a tree planted by the water
   that sends out its roots by the stream.
It does not fear when heat comes;
   its leaves are always green.
It has no worries in a year of drought
   and never fails to bear fruit."

Speak Faith; Silence Sight

Many times we sabotage our outcomes in life by ambushing our faith with words of doubt. We have a natural tendency to speak based on sight and feelings. Our spiritual growth is a maturing process, and it commissions us to retrain our natural senses.

Despite the fact that we use our eyes to see, God wants our faith to be our sight. Eyes of faith look at sickness but see healing. They look at setbacks, but see setups. They look at lack but see abundance, surplus and everlasting increase. They look at confusion but see peace. They look at grief but see joy unspeakable. When you look at your circumstances, what are you seeing?

Let's ask God to lead us to see through eyes of faith, not doubt. Let's ask Him to guard our mouths so that we speak His promises, not the enemy's lies.

2 Corinthians 4:13 - *But having the same spirit of faith, according to what is written, "I believed, therefore I spoke," we also believe, therefore we also speak.* (NASB)

2 Corinthians 5:7 - *For we walk by faith, not by sight.* (NASB)

The Ugly Duckling

Sometimes we go through life with the ugly duckling syndrome. We don't know who we really are because we have a tendency to look at ourselves and our circumstances in the current state. As everything concerning us goes through a maturing process, we tend to think that ugliness is our destiny.

Regardless of our ugly growing stages, we are made in God's magnificent image and are spiritually morphing into the beautiful masterpiece God created us to be. As we grow, our attitudes, patience, compassion and faith may be ugly and underdeveloped, but as we feed on the power and promises of God's Word, we are transformed and mature into the spiritual swan God intended all along.

> **Let's ask God to give us a revelation of who we really are in Him. Let's ask Him to give us a special portion of patience and compassion as others grow and mature. Let's grow past ugly, through Him.**

1 Samuel 16:7 - *But the L*ORD *said to Samuel, "Do not consider his appearance or his height, for I have rejected him. The L*ORD *does not look at the things people look at. People look at the outward appearance, but the L*ORD *looks at the heart."*

1 Peter 2:2-3 - *Like newborn babies, crave pure spiritual milk, so that by it you may grow up in your salvation, now that you have tasted that the Lord is good.*

Healing Awareness

Although October is recognized as a month to support those with cancer and obtain natural intellectual awareness to the importance of screens, annual exams, etc., others are aware of it every day because each day, for them, is a cancer battle. Some may have just been diagnosed, others may be survivors, and this month is a month of testimony to encourage others who are enduring the shock of diagnosis, the weariness of treatment and the fear of death. Whether we are directly affected or know others who are, we are all cancer-aware to some degree. But how many are aware of God's supernatural healing power? How many have faith to believe beyond medicine?

> **Let's intercede for those suffering with cancer. Let's ask God to manifest His healing power over every cell in their body. Let's ask Him to bless doctors with supernatural wisdom and knowledge as they operate for His glory. Let's thank Him in advance for medical miracles, as He manifests Himself in every treatment plan.**

Jeremiah 33:6 - *Behold, I will bring it health and cure, and I will cure them, and will reveal unto them the abundance of peace and truth.* (ASV)

Conquering ALL Through Him

The joy of the Lord is our strength. When we give our issues of life permission to steal our joy, they are also stealing our spiritual, emotional and mental strength. What is it that is trying to distract and oppress your praise and worship?

God manifests Himself in the praises of His people. Through that manifestation comes healing, deliverance, breakthroughs, favor, wisdom and supernatural power. When we welcome a true encounter with God, there is no way we should remain spiritually, naturally, mentally or emotionally stagnant. Your relationships, ministries, health, finances, decisions, businesses, homes, etc., will never be the same when you willfully surrender ALL to God.

Worries of the world can push themselves to the forefront of our minds if we allow them to. Take your spiritual stand today. Reflect on the goodness of God and ALL He has done for you.

Let's ask God to deliver us from demonic distractions that come to steal, kill and destroy our faith. Let's ask Him for a personal and intimate encounter with Him so that we can see the manifestation of His power in everything concerning us. If you are willing, He is able.

Matthew 19:26 - *Jesus looked at them and said, "With man this is impossible, but with God all things are possible."*

Basking in Him

We serve a void-filling God. He has filled emptiness from the beginning of time. He has been the eternal Void Filler, Curse Killer, Spell Breaker, Provider, Healer, Stronghold Puller, Yoke Destroyer and an everlasting Strong Tower to ALL who love Him, serve Him, worship Him, obey Him and glorify Him. If you can even think about how great that is, guess what: HE IS and CAN DO EXCEEDINGLY MORE.

We need a true revelation of God's magnificence. Release your cares to His power. When we finally come to the realization of who God is, what He is, and all the power He has, we will never praise Him with again mental mediocrity. Regardless of what He has done or what we are waiting for Him to do, He's WORTHY of ALL the glory.

> **Let's just ponder God's greatness today and thank Him for being our everlasting Rock. Let's thank Him for His unmerited goodness, mercy and grace. His power is beyond measure, and it resides on the inside of you. Use it for His glory. He's worthy; we're not.**

John 4:23-24 - *Yet a time is coming and has now come when the true worshipers will worship the Father in the Spirit and in truth, for they are the kind of worshipers the Father seeks. God is spirit, and his worshipers must worship in the Spirit and in truth.*

Destiny Despair

As you walk in your divine purpose and toward your divine destiny, you will encounter opposition, struggles, despair and disappointment. It's what we do during those times that molds, strengthens and matures our natural and spiritual character. As we grow spiritually, emotionally and mentally, we should see a shift in our responses to negative situations and negative people.

Don't sink to lower standards to tickle your emotions. Don't take the pressure personally. Everything is working for your good—no matter what it looks like. Just as beauty is skin deep, so is ugly. We have to scratch beyond our sense surface and find the real treasure.

Let's ask God to guard our eyes, ears, minds and emotions as we endure spiritual obstacle courses throughout our journey to greatness in Him. You were built for your battle and created for victory. Live in it!

Ephesians 6:10 - *Finally, be strong in the Lord and in his mighty power.*

Built for Battle and Destined to Win

Today will be as great as you allow it to be. Will you take charge of your day or let it take charge of you? Will you grab your opportunities by the horns, or will you let them charge pass you in a fleeting haze? Will you give your problems permission to be your god today, or will you surrender all to the true God in fierce faith, declaring, commanding, sealing and solidifying His everlasting promises over all that concerns you? Will you hold, or will you fold? Will depression demand your attention, or will you ignore the oppositions of your purpose and peace?

Let's ask God to instill in us an uncompromising spirit of boldness, power and faith. Let's ask Him to deliver us from distractions, decoys and detours of our destiny in Him. You were built for your battle and destined for victory. Command greatness. It's your inheritance. Don't just exist; LIVE in your power.

1 John 5:4 - *For everyone born of God overcomes the world. This is the victory that has overcome the world, even our faith.*

Spiritual Concrete

Many people have their feet planted in spiritual concrete. They are standing stuck. Their eyes are fixed forward on unfinished goals and fertile opportunities, but their steps are locked at a standstill. They are looking ahead but moving nowhere. Is that you today?

What has you planted in a place of spiritual, mental and emotional stagnation? Why haven't you moved forward in years? What is distracting your purpose and pursuit? It's time to chip away at the concrete of captivity. Seeing where you want to go won't get you there unless you start moving.

> **Let's ask God to lead us in putting forth works and action with our faith. Faith is active, are you?**

James 2:17 - *In the same way, faith by itself, if it is not accompanied by action, is dead.*

Change Your World

If you don't like the world you live in, what are you doing about creating a new one? Are you living in green pastures of peace or dead fields of chaos? Do you behold clear skies in your relationships, or is there always a storm brewing? Are you a cloud of thunder or a calm sea? Whatever your world is, you're a part of keeping it alive.

Your world is what you allow it to be, what you speak it to be and what you settle for. If you are tired of life as is, start creating a new one within yourself. Your world starts with God and ends with what you do with His lead.

Let's ask God to encourage us during the anxieties of life. Let's ask Him to strengthen us so that we will not settle for despair and oppression. He is the Creator of all things. Let Him be your Builder as you reconstruct your world. If it's time for change, be a part of it. You have all the tools you need, just use them.

Deuteronomy 20:4 – *For the Lord your God is the one who goes with you to fight for you against your enemies to give you victory.*

John 1:3 - *Through him all things were made; without him nothing was made that has been made.*

Command Your Balance

Living in a world full of fast-paced chaos causes many to feel stressed, over-worked, rest deprived, anxious, spiritually hopeless and emotionally drained. When it seems like there is not enough time in a day, it's usually because every moment is filled with a task. When there is no balance in life, chaos is created.

Some feel as if they are obligated to control everything and everyone and that the world will collapse if they rest. If you are doing more at the expense of your spiritual, mental and physical health, it's time to command peace and balance.

> **Let's ask God to lead us in using our time efficiently and effectively. Let's ask Him to open avenues of peace, balance and rest, as we work for Him. He is the Creator of time, so He knows how to lead us in managing it better.**

Matthew 11:28 - *"Come to me, all you who are weary and burdened, and I will give you rest."* (NKJV)

Spiritual Drought

There are some who are feeling very empty in life. These are the ones who feel as though they are always pouring into others, only to find themselves in a spiritual, emotional and mental drought. Their time, finances, energy, prayer life, hope and relationships feel void and dry.

We all may have encountered a dry season at one time or another. When we feel empty ourselves and yet continue to pour into others, this is when God's latter rains are on the way, and a refreshing overflow is on the horizon. Right when you feel like giving up, your greatest moment is approaching. Be thankful in your emptiness because God is opening you up for more.

Let's ask God to fill every drought in our lives. Whatever it is that feels empty, God is a God of overflow, abundance and provision. He will replenish, restore, refresh and quench every thirst in our lives. An empty vessel can only be filled. When you are empty, then you are open for Him.

Romans 15:13 - *May the God of hope fill you with all joy and peace as you trust in him, so that you may overflow with hope by the power of the Holy Spirit.*

TRANSFORMING IN TRUTH

When we come to the realization that we need a closer relationship with God, we will also realize, even as we draw closer to Him, there are things that will (and should) naturally draw back from us. Our spiritual growth does not have to be forced or done through fleeting religious routine. Growth rooted in truth will transform us naturally at God's personal pace.

During this growing process, there may be seasons of loneliness because familiar people, places and habits may fall away. You will find that God will guard you as you grow, steering you from distractions to your destiny. Don't take the process personal; it's purposeful.

> **Let's ask God to nurture, protect, guide and comfort us through the changes that come with growth in Him. Religion makes you change for people; relationship makes you change for God. Who are you trying to please? You were created to be progressive, not regressive.**

Romans 12:2 - *Do not conform to the pattern of this world, but be transformed by the renewing of your mind. Then you will be able to test and approve what God's will is – His good, pleasing and perfect will.*

You Are a Masterpiece, Not a Mistake

Only you can be you, and only others can be them. When we covet the individuality of others, we are inadvertently telling God He made a mistake in us. Having weaknesses to work on does not mean we are a mistake.

God is not looking for perfection, He is looking for love, faith, truth and obedience. The maturity will follow. Love yourself today through your personal good, bad and ugly. God does not focus on our ugly duckling experiences because He sees the spiritual swan within.

Let's ask God to lead us as we mature and pursue Him in spirit and in truth. Let's ask Him to help us appreciate the uniqueness of our purpose in Him. Don't focus so much on others that you lose sight of your amazing self.

Psalm 119:73-74 - *Your hands made me and formed me; give me understanding to learn Your Commands. May those who fear You rejoice when they see me, for I have put my hope in Your Word.*

DIVINE DETOX

You are full of something that needs to come out. Underneath the distractions, the tiredness, the mistakes, the disappointments, the residue of past pain and heartaches, there is a suppressed gift and purpose that only you possess. When life has hardened your emotions, compassion, zeal and will, it's like spiritual constipation. If we do not do a daily spiritual, emotional and mental cleanse of prayer, pursue our personal peace and release our burdens to God, we clog our spirit with toxins which hinder us from emptying ourselves completely to God's will and way. When our body does not rid itself of waste, it is poisoned in its entirety. If we don't release our spiritual waste, it poisons our spirit.

> **Let's ask God to detox our minds, mouths, emotions and spirits from the waste of worldly worries. May God purge us all through His cleansing power. What are you full of?**

2 Corinthians 7:1 - *Therefore, since we have these promises, dear friends, let us purify ourselves from everything that contaminates body and spirit, perfecting holiness out of reverence for God.*

Titus 3:5 - *He saved us, not because of righteous things we had done, but because of his mercy. He saved us through the washing of rebirth and renewal by the Holy Spirit.*

Faith Fortress

Many of the situations we endure in life damage our mind and emotions. It could be cycles of turbulent relationships, financial misfortune that seems to follow us or some other repetitive cycle that just wears down the mind, body and spirit. When we encounter these lulls in life, we must guard our hearts. Lingering pain flows from our minds to our hearts, then to our mouths, and this opens the door for spiritual bitterness, faithless words and spiritual self-destruction.

Your oppression is not personal. The enemy doesn't need our tangibles. His strategic attacks are about steering our faith away from God. He wants us to question God, question life and question our very purpose. Our love for God and our faith in Him is the breath of our spiritual lives. Don't let the enemy take your wind away from you.

Let's ask God to deliver us from the smothering tactics of the enemy. Faith is our fortress.

Psalm 18:2 - *The Lord is my rock, my fortress and my deliverer;*
my God is my rock, in whom I take refuge,
my shield and the horn of my salvation,
my stronghold.

Hebrews 11:6 - *And without faith it is impossible to please God, because anyone who comes to him must believe that he exists and that he rewards those who earnestly seek him.*

Redirect and Recharge

There are so many times in life that we may make big plans, set big goals and pursue big dreams, only to find that some unforeseen distraction takes the forefront. It could be an unexpected pregnancy, marriage, the death of a loved one, unexpected caregiving responsibilities or some other distracting urgency. When this happens, we can spiral into a zone of unproductive stagnation. And, before you know it, our dreams, goals and plans seem to have faded away in a fog of passing time and expired resources. It's time to redirect, spiritually recharge and let focus become your fortress. Don't lose yourself in the distraction.

Let's ask God to help us bounce back from every unforeseen setback life has thrown our way. Just because life may cause you to pause doesn't mean you have to quit. Keep it moving ... FORWARD.

2 Chronicles 15:7 - *But as for you, be strong and do not give up, for your work will be rewarded.*

Vessels of Victory

How many times have we cried out to God in desperation and when He answered our prayer, our pride wouldn't allow us to accept it? How many times has He used someone to surprisingly bless us, but out of awkwardness and shame, we said "no thank you" or "you didn't have to do that?" Even though God could cause a blessing to just drop out of the sky, usually He uses people as the vessel of our victory.

A seed doesn't sow itself; it needs a sower. Maybe it's a financial burden. Maybe someone needs medicine but has no insurance. Maybe someone has no transportation but has a job they need to get to. Maybe you have lost everything and find yourself needing more than your pride will allow you to admit. Whatever is, don't deny your deliverance when it comes because of pride.

Let's ask God to deliver us from pride. Let's thank Him for open doors and ask Him for the strength to walk through them.

2 Corinthians 8:13-15 - *For I do not mean that others should be eased and you burdened, but that as a matter of fairness your abundance at the present time should supply their need, so that their abundance may supply your need, that there may be fairness. As it is written, "Whoever gathered much had nothing left over, and whoever gathered little had no lack."* (NKJV)

Cycles of Despair

Many times we look for changes in our relationships, finances, health and spiritual growth and wonder why it seems as if we continue to hit the same barriers. Often we are busy looking for the changes to come from the outside when we are the ones who need to make the changes. If you find yourself in cycles of continuous abuse and misuse year after year, season after season, you must ask yourself: what are you doing to change that?

If it's a health issue, what's the eating and exercise cycle? What mental and emotional cycles do we find ourselves in? How do our cycles affect others? What generational cycles are we spinning in?

Let's ask God to give us the wisdom and guidance to break cycles of bondage. We can't expect different results if we keep spinning in the same cycles.

Jeremiah 29:11 - *"For I know the plans I have for you," declares the* LORD, *"plans to prosper you and not to harm you, plans to give you hope and a future."*

Your Best is Yet to Come, So Fight for It

The opposition you are facing is only a tactic to make you give up. The enemy wants to kill your fight, faith, praise, hope and joy. He wants your thoughts to become thoughts of defeat, fear and negativity. He wants you to stop believing in the goodness of others and the faithfulness of God.

You will NOT give up today! If you have fallen, YOU WILL GET UP. Your fight is not just for you; it's to keep your purpose alive because once you rise, you will pull others up too. It's not just about us; our victory banners are a light to those who are also in despair. When you win, your victory gives others the faith to pull themselves up and keep fighting. Therefore, when you feel like throwing in the towel, that's when you must dig deeper into the promises of God and bring Him in remembrance of what He has commanded to be yours.

Let's ask God to renew our strength in times of despair. Your best is yet to come, so fight for it!

Psalm 28:7-9 - *The Lord is my strength and my shield;*
my heart trusts in Him, and He helps me.
My heart leaps for joy,
and with my song I praise Him.

The Serenity of Solitude

Sometimes the bustle of life steals our peace, individuality and intimate prayer time. Some have gotten so used to being tasking robots that there almost seems to be nothing more to life than mundane routine. Whether it's the responsibility of marriage, single parenthood, multiple jobs or just the frantic unforeseen day-to-day upsets, we are individuals who require time to love self, rest ourselves and seek God for ourselves.

Command your moment. Take time to find a place of peace today with just you and God.

Let's ask God to lead us to a place and time of solitude, peace and prayer in the midst of life, love and living. Let's ask Him to lead us in managing our time so that we never leave Him out of the days He has blessed us with. Let's pray for balance in our mind and emotions. Jesus often found serenity in prayerful solitude. Have you found yours?

Luke 5:16 - *But Jesus often withdrew to lonely places and prayed.*

Redirect from Doubt to Faith

Sometimes we can become so desperate that we began to worship our resources rather than our Source. The enemy knows we have tangible needs that sometimes can't wait, so our focus of desperation takes our eyes off of God. If you are in this desperate place, remind yourself that God is all, is in all and controls all.

Don't let the quick fix fool you. When we find ourselves obsessing over our lack, we need to refocus and redirect our faith to God's eternal promises. He's a no-limit God. Every resource has a cap, but there is no cap, ceiling or lack in God. He is infinite, eternal, everlasting, more than enough, and He never runs out of benefits or blessings. Let's get connected and redirected.

Let's ask God to renew our strength and encourage our faith as we believe Him for what seems impossible. Let's ask Him to lead us to our overflow, abundance and favor. God opens doors man cannot shut.

---

2 Corinthians 9:8 - *And God is able to bless you abundantly, so that in all things at all times, having all that you need, you will abound in every good work.*

Seal, Secure and Solidify Your Blessing

Do not give up on your breakthrough. Some are so weary and on the verge of throwing in the spiritual, natural and mental towel that despair has become their companion. Today lift your head and lift your voice and speak your breakthrough.

If you have received an eviction notice, repossession notice, bad health report, a message of financial ruin or any other negative report, look at the report and declare, decree, secure and solidify that no matter what appears to be ruin is renewal. Declare that your joy is unspeakable, your peace surpasses understanding and your lack is a vacant vessel of pending overflow.

We serve a God of supernatural supply. You will not lose; you win. You do not lack; you have more than enough. You will not fail; you are victory. Your present despair is not your destiny.

Let's thank God for the miraculous. Let's ask Him to supernaturally derail every plot of the enemy to distract our faith. You possess power. Activate it.

2 Timothy 1:7 - *For God has not given us a spirit of fear, but of power and of love and of a sound mind.* (NKJV)

Ephesians 6:10 - *Finally, my brethren, be strong in the Lord, and in the power of His might.* (NKJV)

Birth Your Purpose

We are all pregnant with purpose, but we must labor in order to deliver. Do not get frustrated with your process. Do not give up on what God has entrusted to come forth through you. Don't give up during your pushing season. See what others have done in your area of purpose and connect with excellence.

Your purpose is alive, thriving and ready to come forth. Some feel like giving up on their dreams and purpose because they feel as if they do not have the resources to bring their vision forth. If God gave you the vision, He will make the provision.

Let's ask God to lead us to the resources of His choice that will be our spiritual midwives as we labor to bring forth our purpose in Him. Let's ask Him for perseverance and patience as our purpose shines for His glory. What are you carrying?

John 15:16 - *You did not choose me, but I chose you and appointed you so that you might go and bear fruit – fruit that will last – and so that whatever you ask in my name the Father will give you.*

Our Unchanging Changer

Because we live in a world of constant and unpredictable change, it is imperative that we establish an intimate and personal relationship with our never-changing God. People may change in the way they treat you, respond to you or love you. Circumstances may change with regards to health, finances, relationships and employment conditions. Our nation may even change with regards to leadership, foreign relations and unity. The one remaining constant that can change anything, yet remains stable, consistent and eternally reliable is our All-Powerful God.

If you find yourself lost in the chaos of disappointment in people, things and personal set-backs, lift your head and your heart toward our everlasting God. He is our Haven of Peace and our Shelter of Comfort, no matter what. You are not forgotten or forsaken.

Let's thank God that when all else fails, He never will. Let's thank Him for being our Rock and Fortress when all else crumbles. Stay connected to Him.

Numbers 23:19 - *God is not human, that he should lie,*
   not a human being, that he should change his mind.
   Does he speak and then not act?
   Does he promise and not fulfill?

Hebrews 13:8 - *Jesus Christ is the same yesterday and today and forever.*

James 1:17 - *Every good and perfect gift is from above, coming down from the Father of the heavenly lights, who does not change like shifting shadows.*

The Opposition of Oppression

When you feel lost, alone, betrayed and forgotten, let it be a powerful reminder that God is your Keeper and Guide, and His eyes stay on you. When you feel you have been blocked, pushed to the back of life's line and overlooked, know that God is the One who gave you purpose and power, and nothing and no one can stop your life's assignment. Your season to be catapulted is on the horizon.

Remind yourself that God is the opposite of everything you are enduring, and He has a promise for every problem. The only thing that can hold you down is your belief that something can. God would not give anything enough power to stop His purpose in you. Your purpose is personal to God.

Let's ask God to give us patience and guidance as He perfects His work in us. Nothing can minimize the max God put in you.

Job 42:2 - *I know that you can do all things;*
no purpose of yours can be thwarted.

The Pains of Plan and Purpose

God reigns High above our thoughts. His ways are not our ways, and His thoughts are not our thoughts. He takes the foolish things to baffle the wise and what the enemy means for evil, God can transform for good. He has a purpose for everything under the sun, and it is ALL working out for the good of those who love Him.

Whatever God allows, He has a plan and purpose for it. Trust, believe, watch and pray, and see the salvation of our God in all that concerns you. It's time to get spiritually independent and take a time-out for just riding on the strength of others. If we ever needed to know God for ourselves, it's now.

> *Let's ask God to heal the land and all who dwell in it. Let's pray for a spiritual awakening and a miraculous revival of faith, hope, unity and peace. Let's pray that this nation does not just have a form of unity and yet continue to deny the power of it. Jesus rose for everything that is going on in our world, so let's not keep Him buried. If you do, don't complain about the whirlwind.*

Proverbs 29:2 - *When the righteous are in authority, the people rejoice; But when a wicked man rules, the people groan.* (NKJV)

2 Corinthians 8:14 - *At the present time your plenty will supply what they need, so that in turn their plenty will supply what you need. The goal is equality.*

Proverbs 27:20 - *Death and Destruction are never satisfied, and neither are human eyes.*

Battle Season

During these critical and turbulent times, we need to operate by the power of God's anointing, not just by worldly knowledge and flesh. It is time-out for religious routine as usual. We need to pray, fast and seek God for direction and navigation through the maze of world turmoil.

It's time-out for mundane church programs. It's time for miracles, signs and wonders. It's time to let God order our steps and lead us in bringing others to a knowledge of His truth, as we pray and seek His face for our personal role in world change. Just because we have a voice does not mean we have the power of God backing it up.

Let's pray for God's anointing to manifest in all that concerns us. Let's ask Him to transform hearts of stone into hearts of flesh. Let's ask Him to empty us of self so that we can be full of Him. Let's ask Him to deliver all leaders from the spirit of pride because we know pride precedes great falls. Let's thank Him for preparing the way, as we invite Him in with a spirit of truth.

Proverbs 16:18 - *Pride goes before destruction, a haughty spirit before a fall.*

Ezekiel 36:26 - *I will give you a new heart and put a new spirit in you; I will remove from you your heart of stone and give you a heart of flesh.*

Harvest Time

In a world of curve balls and hard balls, setbacks and letdowns, we can get so caught up in our needs and wants that we forget to give thanks for what we already have. We can become so focused on our lack that we become blind to the many things we do have.

Today let's reflect on our sufficiency. Despite what we feel we do not have, we have so much to be thankful for. Let's reflect on the fact that we have life, a new day with new opportunities to make today better than yesterday, we have God and an opportunity to get to know Him better.

Let's give God thanks for all He has done for us over the course of our blessed lives. More than anything, let's thank Him for Who He is, not just for what He did, does and will do. Whatever it is you are waiting for God to manifest, sow into the ground you want to reap from. Your harvest season is on the way.

2 Corinthians 9:6-8 - *Remember this: Whoever sows sparingly will also reap sparingly, and whoever sows generously will also reap generously. Each of you should give what you have decided in your heart to give, not reluctantly or under compulsion, for God loves a cheerful giver. And God is able to bless you abundantly, so that in all things at all times, having all that you need, you will abound in every good work.*

See Yourself Magnified, Not Minuscule

Let's ask God to lead us in being doers, not just hearers and watchers in life. Sometimes we lose sight of our potential because we sit dormant in fear thinking that we are very minuscule in the big scheme of life. There is nothing minuscule about us in God's eyes. He sees us through eyes of spiritual magnification. He sees our expanded purpose, while our view of ourselves is sometimes blurred with self-doubt.

Let's ask God to deliver us from self-doubt and fear. Let's ask Him to expand our personal view so we can see past our shortcomings, limits and past mistakes. The only ceiling we have is the one we create.

Jeremiah 29:11-13 - *"For I know the plans I have for you," declares the* LORD, *"plans to prosper you and not to harm you, plans to give you hope and a future. Then you will call on me and come and pray to me, and I will listen to you. You will seek me and find me when you seek me with all your heart."*

Decisions

Decision-making is one of the most important aspects of our spiritual and natural walk. Because our decisions mold our lives, we want to patiently make the best decisions we possibly can. Many times bad decisions are made due to impatience. We sometimes want instant gratification, quick answers and instant results, so we have a tendency to prematurely make quick and hasty decisions. Bad decisions often have long-term impacts.

> **Let's ask God to deliver us from impatience and premature decision-making. Let's ask Him to guide us in using wisdom instead of impulse.**

Proverbs 3:6 - *In all your ways submit to him, and he will make your paths straight.*

James 1:5 - *If any of you lacks wisdom, you should ask God, who gives generously to all without finding fault, and it will be given to you.*

The Gift of Giving

Whatever skills, gifts, and talents God has blessed us with, we must always remember to give Him all the honor. We are given gifts to share with the world, not keep for ourselves. However, we are to share these gifts with a spirit of humility and modesty, not arrogance or pride.

God is the One who gives us worth and value. No matter how good, gifted, smart or successful we are, it's all to God's glory, not ours. Our best is only a glimpse of His greatness.

Let's ask God to keep us humble in our accomplishments. Let's ask Him to give us a heart of praise and worship as we reflect on His Perfect Power. Let's remember that we can do all things through Him, but are nothing without Him.

1 Corinthians 4:7 - *For who makes you different from anyone else? What do you have that you did not receive? And if you did receive it, why do you boast as though you did not?*

Faith-Focus

Being a devout martial artist, I was always trained to hit through a target. Surface focus minimizes power, but if you aim well beyond your target, your power will amaze you. This taught me focus.

What are your eyes fixed on? Your life follows your focus. Whatever you stare at is where your mind, heart and energy will stay. If you are staring at your present circumstance, you will find yourself taking residence there. Don't stare at where you are; focus on where you want to be, and you will arrive. If you are in a valley, don't keep your eyes fixed on your fall. Look to the hills and mountain tops of victory, deliverance, prosperity and healing. Let's ask God to redirect our focus.

Let's ask God to redirect our focus. Let's ask Him to remove every distraction of doubt that tries to blur our faith-focus. Believe past your problem, and you will make contact with your destiny. Hit life with the fist of faith.

---

1 Corinthians 2:5 - *so that your faith might not rest on human wisdom, but on God's power.*

Your Breaking Point Is Your Strongest Point

Some have endured so many back-to-back hits from life that they feel they are now at a mental, emotional, and physical breaking point. I want to encourage the stressed, pressed and shaken today. No matter how shattered you may feel, you are not broken. You may be hard hit, but as long as you have breath, you have fight left in you.

The beautiful thing about the fights we face is that our battles are already won. We just have to catch up with our victory. We sometimes have to go through the mental motions, but the spiritual battle is won. When you feel that you are at your breaking point, you are actually at your strongest point. In your weakest hours, God's power is manifested. When you are weakest, He is strongest.

Let's ask God to deliver us from a broken mindset. Let's ask Him to undergird us with His peace that surpasses all understanding and His everlasting comfort.

---

2 Corinthians 4:8-9 - *We are hard pressed on every side, but not crushed; perplexed, but not in despair; persecuted, but not abandoned; struck down, but not destroyed.*

2 Corinthians 12:9-10 - *But he said to me, "My grace is sufficient for you, for my power is made perfect in weakness." Therefore I will boast all the more gladly about my weaknesses, so that Christ's power may rest on me. That is why, for Christ's sake, I delight in weaknesses, in insults, in hardships, in persecutions, in difficulties. For when I am weak, then I am strong.*

Raise Your Bar

Sometimes, when relationships and/or marriages fail, those involved can be left feeling depressed, guilty and lonely. They can grow comfortable in a shell of isolation, feeling safe and secure, yet alone and weary. Others may find themselves staying in damaging and abusive relationships, for fear of loneliness and broken self-worth. Don't let insecurity lower your standards, and never settle for less than your worth.

When you know your value and respect the value in others, you will never shrink yourself to make others feel big, and you will never shrink others to expand yourself.

> *Let's ask God to lead us in loving ourselves and others according to His will. Let's ask Him to heal every broken heart and mind that has been damaged by self-doubt, insecurity and fear. Let's ask Him to mature us in knowing the difference between love and passion. Let's ask Him to rescue those who have become comfortable with pain.*

1 John 4:18 - *There is no fear in love. But perfect love drives out fear, because fear has to do with punishment. The one who fears is not made perfect in love.*

The Power of Positivity

There is power in positivity. No matter how negative your situation is at this time, your attitude can make all the difference in your comeback. This year has been a challenge for many, due to natural disasters, tragedy, loss and death. When the depression of your oppression hits you hard, it's time to command a spiritual, mental and emotional redirection. You have to command your joy, when the enemy tries to command your demise. When life redirects your hopes, plans and dreams, it's time to redirect your faith.

Let's ask God to redirect us from the temporary to the eternal. Let's ask Him for patience, peace and joy during spiritual, mental and physical setbacks. Let's thank Him for reminding us that all things are possible through Him when all we see is impossible. Your restoration is reaching for you. Embrace it.

Job 42:10 - *After Job had prayed for his friends, the LORD restored his fortunes and gave him twice as much as he had before.*

Dirty Glasses of Depression

Depression is like dirty glasses; it distorts what's ahead in life through a blurry haze that makes purpose, joy, peace and destiny look like a fog of unrecognizable illusions. It makes thoughts of suicide seem like the only clear vision ahead. That blur is a trick of the enemy to distort your personal destiny and purpose that only your life can bring forth. Take those glasses off today, so you can see what God says about you. Begin to speak, command and declare His promises over your life and circumstances.

> *Let's pray for those who suffer with depression. Let's ask God to heal the heartbreak of those who have lost loved ones to depression and suicide. Let's ask Him to heal their minds of the torment of unanswered questions and guilt. Let your view of life be what God wants you to see.*

Jeremiah 29:11 - *"For I know the plans I have for you," declares the LORD, "plans to prosper you and not to harm you, plans to give you hope and a future."*

John 16:33 - *"I have told you these things, so that in me you may have peace. In this world you will have trouble. But take heart! I have overcome the world."*

Drop Your Weights

Seasons sometimes come in life when you may feel spiritually desolate and emotionally disconnected. Maybe the baggage of past circumstances you have carried for so long has finally gotten too heavy. Maybe you have just fought so hard for so long that you just feel spiritually, mentally, emotionally and physically exhausted.

We were not created to carry yokes, even though we can. Your purpose is not to struggle and be weary. You were created to have power and dominion over your areas of influence. Do not give up on the manifestation of your victory.

Let's ask God to renew our strength. Let's release the burdens, yokes and weights that try to weigh us down and distract our destiny. God is bigger than your burden.

Psalm 55:22 - *Cast your cares on the Lord*
and he will sustain you;
he will never let
the righteous be shaken.

Love Conquers and Covers

There is nothing like the feeling of being shown love when you miss a mark of expectation. There is nothing like opened arms of love when life seems to turn its back and fold its arms against us. Many people are shunned, overlooked and ignored because of mistakes they may have made. Where would we be if God did not love us through our shortcomings, mistakes, bad decisions and mishaps?

How much better would a person feel if they were encouraged to get up, dust themselves off and get back in their race. You never lose until you quit! So love on someone today. Encourage someone in their purpose today. Love someone past their imperfections, faults and setbacks. God didn't ignore, shun or write us off. He loves us in spite of ourselves.

Let's ask God to perfect His work in us. Let's ask Him to transform our hearts of stone into hearts of flesh. Let's show to others the love that has been shown to us.

1 Peter 4:8 - *Above all, love each other deeply, because love covers over a multitude of sins.*

Fleshly-Led vs. Spiritually-Guided

Sometimes, when the chaos of life throws us into a whirlwind, instead of spinning with a spiral, we have to be still. Being still is not always easy, when decisions are time-sensitive, outcomes are unexpected and the unforeseen strikes with a vengeance. Just as arguing results in a more intense confrontation, being chaotic during chaos keeps the chaos going.

Confusion feeds off of itself. We have to oppose the opposition. Be still and know that God is God, and He has ALL power. He is all-knowing and ever-present, so our answers exist, and they will manifest in God's timing, not ours. Declare that you will overcome the press of life. Your peace will come, and your joy will be renewed. You will not lack, and you will not remain lost.

Let's ask God to calm our storms, redirect our paths and renew our strength. Let's ask Him to lead us in being still so that He can move. God doesn't need our help; He needs our obedience.

Mark 11:22-24 - *"Have faith in God," Jesus answered. "Truly I tell you, if anyone says to this mountain, 'Go, throw yourself into the sea,' and does not doubt in their heart but believes that what they say will happen, it will be done for them.' Therefore I tell you, whatever you ask for in prayer, believe that you have received it, and it will be yours."*

Deflect the Destiny Distractors

There are some things that come to the forefront of your life to distract your destiny. It could be the distraction of a sour relationship, a sense of spiritual shifting, the waywardness of a child, circumstantial hardships, health issues or just a phantom frustration that seems to have no real root. Whatever it WAS, you will deflect the destiny distractors today. Destiny distractions come to take your eyes off of purpose so you can focus on pain. The enemy of your destiny knows you have purpose, but he comes to cause you to lose hope in fulfilling it. You were not created with purpose to not fulfill it.

Let's ask God to deliver us from spiritual, mental and emotional distractions. He is perfecting everything concerning you. You may not understand where you are today, but your path has purpose.

Proverbs 16:9 - *In their hearts humans plan their course, but the Lord establishes their steps.*

God Is Not a Second-Fiddle God

There has been such a horrible rise in domestic violence, murder-suicides and relational dysfunction. This is because some lose sight of who God really is, allowing people and relationships to become idols. God is not a second-fiddle God. He is a ONE AND ONLY GOD. He wants to be first in all that we do and have.

In relationships, God wants to be the Center, Counsel and Balance. In our needs, He wants to be acknowledged as our Sole Provider. In our confusion, He wants to be our Peace. In our mistakes and shortcomings, He wants to be our Redeemer and Savior. In our sickness, He wants to be our Healer.

When we put people, places and things before God, mayhem is sure to follow. Sure, God provides us with resources, but He wants to always be recognized as our Source. Nothing and no one can be Who God is to us.

Let's ask God to be our ALL in everything. Let's ask Him to give us divine balance in all that concerns us. Even though He knows that He is number one, He wants us to make His status personal.

John 1:3 - *Through him all things were made; without him nothing was made that has been made.*

Purpose in Your Pain

There is a blessing in your burden. No matter what we face under the mud is a miracle. God created us to progress and grow naturally and spiritually. Most living things that develop, mature and grow go through various phases, and our spirituality is no different. We morph from one phase to another, destined to grow in God's grace.

However, during our seasons of growth, there is sometimes pain. Growing causes us to stretch, expand and press beyond our comfort zones—physically, mentally and spiritually. Embrace your next today. You have purpose and promise.

Let's ask God to give us a spirit of vigilance and patience as we grow in Him. Your discomfort has destiny.

Philippians 1:6 - *Being confident of this, that he who began a good work in you will carry it on to completion until the day of Christ Jesus.*

New Day

New Year's is a time when many declare they want to lose weight and begin a spiritual and physical detox. For those counting the pounds they want to lose or the extra baggage they want to drop, start with shedding the pounds and bags of negativity. Some are spiritually obese with no balance. Some are living life full of toxic people, unhealthy relationships and destiny-distracting places and things. Some carry pounds of addictive behaviors, only finding that they have just shed one addiction to gain another. Command your year to line up with victory, renewal, revival and restoration. This year, when you fall off of your plan of purpose, jump back on immediately. Don't let it be another annual defeat of all you desire to overcome and become.

Let's ask God to guide us each step of our victorious path as we live in His power.

Isaiah 43:18-19 - *Forget the former things;*
do not dwell on the past.
See, I am doing a new thing!
Now it springs up; do you not perceive it?
I am making a way in the wilderness
and streams in the wasteland.

There Must Be Discipline Before Destiny

Embrace today with an expectation of all you need and desire, according to God's perfect will. Sometimes we get confused with regards to our wants and needs. Some may desperately want to be married or be in a long-lasting relationship with promise, but God may know you NEED to let go of some baggage and get to know HIM and yourself better before trying to know someone else.

Some may be wondering why they can't receive the abundant financial overflow. Maybe God is trying to make you faithful over a little before entrusting you with a lot.

Let's ask God to lead us and impart His wisdom in us as we grow and mature in our purpose. Let's pray to be Spirit-guided not flesh-directed.

Proverbs 12:1 - *Whoever loves discipline loves knowledge, but whoever hates correction is stupid.*

Renew and Reset

Renew your mind and reset your vision. What you think is what you will allow to become your reality. Our mind is the stomping ground of the enemy and, as long as we leave the ground fertile for his feet, he will send a mirage of defeat, doubt and low self-esteem. Renew your mind by filling it with what God declares for your life. Once you start putting truth in your mind, the lie of the evil one will vanish.

> **Let's ask God to wash our minds with the promises of His Words of truth. Let's ask Him to heal us from every mental scar and open wound. Your mind is a beautiful thing so don't let the ugly invade.**

Romans 12:2 - *Do not conform to the pattern of this world, but be transformed by the renewing of your mind. Then you will be able to test and approve what God's will is — His good, pleasing and perfect will.*

Philippians 4:8 - *Finally, brothers and sisters, whatever is true, whatever is noble, whatever is right, whatever is pure, whatever is lovely, whatever is admirable — if anything is excellent or praiseworthy — think about such things.*

The Predators of Your Peace

It's time to slay the predators of your peace, which are confusion, doubt, low self-esteem, negativity and fear. These predators come to steal your dreams, visions, hopes and purpose. They come in the form of people, places, things and thoughts to make you doubt yourself, your abilities and your gifts and distract your assignment. You are a power-house of purpose. The only thing hindering you is your doubt in yourself and your doubt in God's promises. He said you were created for His purpose before you were even born. The world has been waiting for your ordained arrival. Now you're here!

Let's ask God to deny the distractions of our destiny in Him. Let's ask Him to manifest the fullness of His power in all that concerns us. Watch your giants fall as you rise.

---

2 Timothy 1:9 - *He has saved us and called us to a holy life – not because of anything we have done but because of his own purpose and grace. This grace was given us in Christ Jesus before the beginning of time.*

The Supernatural Power of Prayer

The power of prayer is not just some religious cliché; it's a fact. There is supernatural power in prayer, and it does miraculously change things. It's the antidote for evil, hardship, confusion, lost paths, misguidance, pain, rejection and grief. Prayer is a wall and a rock.

Walk in prayer today. Don't just let your day guide you; guide your day. As soon as our eyes open, we realize we are still alive. We have a new day with a new mission. Cover your mission with prayer.

Let's ask God to navigate us today. Let's ask Him to lead us in divine order and purpose. Let's ask Him to lead us in peace, excellence and obedience. Release your life to prayer and watch God release you to power.

Colossians 4:2 - *Devote yourselves to prayer, being watchful and thankful.*

No Weapon

It's not the limits of others that holds us back; it's our own limits. Yes, people can try to block your destiny, purpose and commission in life, but it's up to us to seek God for His deliverance and guidance. All we have to do is take everything to God in faith-filled prayer.

If you feel lost, ask God to guide you. If you feel oppressed, ask God to deliver you. If you feel you are being misjudged, mistreated, hindered and blocked, ask God to vindicate you and direct you to paths of favor and wisdom.

Nothing can stop God's will for your life. Sometimes we are right where we need to be that so God can align us where we are supposed to be. Your now is only a preparation season for your Next.

Let's ask God to transform our self-doubt into self-assurance. Your now-place has purpose.

Isaiah 54:17 - *No weapon formed against you shall prosper,*
And every tongue which rises against you in judgment
You shall condemn.
This is the heritage of the servants of the Lord,
And their righteousness is from Me,"
  says the Lord. (NKJV)

Lift the Leaders and Lift the Land

The oppression of people for ages has occurred when authorities are fleshly led instead of spiritually guided. The spirit that rules the authorities is the spirit that tries to reign. From the home to the workplace, to the church and nation, the one in charge sets the atmosphere. This is the reason we are to pray for those who lead, parent, teach, supervise, pastor and govern. Talking about a problem, person or circumstance does very little, but prayer has power to do anything. It's God who has the heart of man in the palm of His hand, and He alone can turn a pharaoh's heart of stone into a heart of flesh, not us.

Let's lift up those in authority today. Let's ask God to lead every leader according to His will and purpose. Let's ask Him to lead us all in truth, love, and wisdom. Let's ask Him to protect all leaders from the destructive spirits of pride, arrogance and confusion. As we are told to submit to authorities, let's ask God to lead the authorities in submitting to Him. In all that we submit to, let's pray for righteous rule.

2 Chronicles 7:14 - *If my people, who are called by my name, will humble themselves and pray and seek my face and turn from their wicked ways, then I will hear from heaven, and I will forgive their sin and will heal their land.*

Proverbs 28:2 - *When a country is rebellious, it has many rulers, but a ruler with discernment and knowledge maintains order.*

Proverbs 29:2 - *When the righteous thrive, the people rejoice; when the wicked rule, the people groan.*

Forgive to Be Forgiven

The baggage of grudges weighs more than your spirit can bear. Unforgiveness is like a toxic spiritual infection that eats away at your peace, mind, body and spirit. It eventually chews through your heart and then begins to manifest itself as sickness in your spirit, mind and body. It severs ties between families, friends, co-workers, churches and communities and spreads from region to region, poisoning other relationships by putting those who have nothing to do with the cause of the dissension in awkward situations.

The root of unforgiveness is pain and pride. What do you have to lose today if you forgive? How hard is it to break the years of silence? What difference does it make who reaches out first? When you release others, your release yourself. Forgiveness is power.

Let's ask God to soften and heal every callous heart that has been broken and betrayed. Let's ask Him to help us forgive others as He has forgiven us.

Mark 11:25 - *And when you stand praying, if you hold anything against anyone, forgive them, so that your Father in heaven may forgive you your sins.*

1 John 1:9 - *If we confess our sins, he is faithful and just and will forgive us our sins and purify us from all unrighteousness.*

Matthew 6:15 - *But if you do not forgive others their sins, your Father will not forgive your sins.*

Live in Spirit and in Truth

How do we glorify God? It's more than just raised hands and a shout on Sunday morning. How do we glorify Him on the rest of the days of our week? We glorify Him by being like Him. In order to do that, we sometimes have to go against our own grain. Sometimes we have to take the high road when the low road is most comfortable. It's easy to repay evil with evil and unkindness with a taste of itself, but we are called to be a light in darkness, not shade in the shadows.

Challenge yourself today. Whatever it is that has been pressing your patience, love and peace, ask God to soften your heart and change your attitude and perspective. Sometimes our focus on the opposition causes us to lose sight of ourselves and who God has called us to be.

Let's ask God to harness our flesh and lead us as we represent His goodness and mercy in a merciless world. Let's ask Him to heal every callous and stubborn heart. If He treated us like we treat each other, where would we be?

John 15:12 - *"My command is this: Love each other as I have loved you."*

Ephesians 4:32 - *Be kind and compassionate to one another, forgiving each other, just as in Christ God forgave you.*

The Personal Prisoner

Sometimes we are prisoner of our own limits and chains. We are so used to facing limiting words that our minds and spirits can become a haven of doubt. We are conditioned to think we don't have enough money, potential, favor and opportunity because the enemy of this world has misaligned us with what God says. It's time for a spiritual alignment.

We serve a God who has all, is all and is in all. Do you think He created all things and yet lacks in anything? Whatever we need, God has it. Let's ask Him to lead us in taking the limits off of our faith in Him. Faith comes through relationship with Him and getting to know His Word and what He says about us.

Let's stop speaking what the enemy says about us and start speaking what our all-powerful God says. Let's ask God to renew our minds and remove our doubt. The only true lack we have is faith.

Romans 10:17 - *So then faith comes by hearing, and hearing by the word of God.* (NKJV)

Ephesians 4:6 - *One God and Father of all, who is over all and through all and in all.* (NKJV)

Forward Faith

Be reminded today that whatever it is you are going through is not your final destination, unless you chose to reside there. Your oppression is not destined to be your homeland. Life brings us through many journeys, but keep your steps moving forward. Don't settle for the valley, even though you may be going through one. Always keep your eyes and head up because once you start focusing on your low place, you will remain there. Our challenges demand our focus, but don't follow your focus if it's locked in on the wrong place.

> *Let's ask God to lead us as we trod through valley terrain. Let's ask Him to lead us in being faith-focused, so we won't be blinded by doubt. Your focus has power, so use it wisely.*

Proverbs 4:25 – *Let your eyes look straight ahead; fix your gaze directly before you.*

Proverbs 16:3 - *Commit to the Lord whatever you do, and He will establish your plans.*

Colossians 3:2 - *Set your minds on things above, not on earthly things.*

Patience Through Pain

There are some who are going through what I call the Why Syndrome. They are wondering why it seems like everything they try to do goes wrong. Why is it that no matter how hard they try to make their marriage work, the enemy seems to have their spouse going in the opposite direction? Why does it seem like no matter how hard they try to raise their children to be respectful they are rude and have a spirit of entitlement? Why is it the job never comes through? When your spirit is full of questions, know that God's timing is perfect. Sometimes what we want is not what we need when we want it. God has a plan for your life, and it's not necessarily the plan He has for others. If we had what others had when we wanted it, it could be a disaster for us. Only God knows the beginning from the end, not us. He knows the outcome of a thing, while we are still praying for the beginning of it.

Let's ask God to give us patience and faith as we go through seasons of pain, questions and doubt. Trouble doesn't last forever, but God's faithfulness does.

James 1:2-4 - *Consider it pure joy, my brothers and sisters, whenever you face trials of many kinds, because you know that the testing of your faith produces perseverance. Let perseverance finish its work so that you may be mature and complete, not lacking anything.*

The War on Love

To those who are finding that their relationships are under attack, let me tell you why. It's not about your relationship; it's about the love in it. The enemy of your soul wants to have an affair with you. He is jealous of the love in your life, especially your love for God. He wants to sabotage your bond with God and distract you with the lust of doubt, fear and insecurity. He wants you to focus on him. He begs for your attention through his delicacies of anger, confusion, division, strife, selfishness and abuse. If you pay too much attention to God, the enemy will attack your next closest relationships. Separate yourself from him through prayer, faith and focus.

> Let's ask God to sever our ties with the enemy's tactics. Let's thank God for His secure love, protection and deliverance. Let's ask Him to seal, secure and solidify His love bond with us. Let's ask Him to teach us real love so we won't live in self-defined love. God is a faithful God, so don't cheat on Him with the enemy.

Luke 10:27 - *He answered, " 'Love the Lord your God with all your heart and with all your soul and with all your strength and with all your mind'; and, 'Love your neighbor as yourself.' "*

The Seasonal Steward

Many feel as though they are struggling and living off of financial crumbs, sustaining themselves on just enough. No matter how rich, poor or financially mediocre you feel, God can miraculously do more with less. He's done it since the beginning of time. He will fill your voids supernaturally because He a God of abundance, overflow and infinite provision.

Sometimes it's not what we don't have; it's what we are doing with what we do have. Sometimes we don't need more money; we need better stewardship. God will lead us in being a steward over a little so that we can manage the overflow in our seasons of increase.

> Let's ask God to encourage those who feel poverty stricken and financially desperate. Let's ask Him to lead us in wisdom in being better stewards over our blessings. You don't lack when you serve a God who has all.

Haggai 2:8 – *"The silver is mine and the gold is mine," declares the Lord Almighty.*

Philippians 4:19 - *And my God will meet all your needs according to the riches of His glory in Christ Jesus.*

The Power of God's Undergirding

You will not release any power to your adversary today. Nothing will steal your joy, peace, love or patience. You will walk in authority today, and you will stand in victory. The oppressor of your soul, mind and spirit will fold and flee. God will surround you with those who need to be in your space and scatter those who do not.

It's time to claim your ground and cover every area of your life by asking God to under-gird your home, family, friends and loved ones. You will no longer try so hard to force your way into being accepted where you are now rejected because sometimes rejection from the right place is protecting God's best interests for your life. You are loved, victorious, prosperous and at peace. Favor finds you.

Let's ask God to manifest His best for our lives and give us the revelation of recognizing it.

---

2 Thessalonians 3:3 - *But the Lord is faithful, and He will strengthen you and protect you from the evil one.*

Fair-Weather Faith

When we want to see our world align with victory in every area, we must make sure our faith, works and words line up with what we are believing God for. His promises don't change, but our faith and words often do. God is not a fair-weather God, so let's not walk in fair-weather faith or speak fair-weather words.

> Let's ask God to reveal His power in our faith-filled declarations. Let's ask Him to strengthen us when we are tempted to walk by sight. Don't speak dead words over living promises.

Hebrews 4:12 - *For the word of God is alive and active. Sharper than any double-edged sword, it penetrates even to dividing soul and spirit, joints and marrow; it judges the thoughts and attitudes of the heart.*

Motive vs. Money

Whether it be tithes, offerings, time or gracious community servitude, when it comes to being a giver, we must realize we are not doing God any favors. Let's not be confused; God does not need our money. The whole Earth is His and the fullness of it, so He is the totality of what we need. He is the fullness of all empty things. He doesn't need a big bank; He needs big hearts.

All we have is because of God, so let's remember Him in our giving and be generous. In the same cheerful spirit we graciously receive the blessings of God, let's be just as graciously cheerful in our giving. It's not about how much we give; it's about the heart from which we give. God honors the motive, not the money.

Let's ask God to lead us in having motives that line up with His will and Word.

Matthew 6:2-4 - *So when you give to the needy, do not announce it with trumpets, as the hypocrites do in the synagogues and on the streets, to be honored by others. Truly I tell you, they have received their reward in full. But when you give to the needy, do not let your left hand know what your right hand is doing, so that your giving may be in secret. Then your Father, who sees what is done in secret, will reward you.*

2 Corinthians 9:7 - *Each of you should give what you have decided in your heart to give, not reluctantly or under compulsion, for God loves a cheerful giver.*

1 Timothy 6:17-18 - *Command those who are rich in this present world not to be arrogant nor to put their hope in wealth, which is so uncertain, but to put their hope in God, who richly provides us with everything for our enjoyment. Command them to do good, to be rich in good deeds, and to be generous and willing to share.*

Unconditional Gratitude

When you are at the mountain top of peace in the home with peace in your relationships, abundance in your finances, receiving unmerited favor, having open doors of opportunity and supernatural turnaround, remember God's power with a spirit of gratitude. When you are in the valleys of confusion in the home, enduring wayward family, contrary children, strained relationships, workplace chaos, unemployment, empty bank accounts or poor health reports, remember that God's power never fails or falters. Even when you feel empty, let God know you are grateful because His power doesn't stop in your valley; it's building your mountain.

In whatever season we are in, let's not only give a thank you; let's LIVE a thank you. Let thankfulness and gratitude be a lifestyle offering to God at all times. Give thanks out of your emptiness, and watch God fill you up.

Ephesians 3:17-19 - *So that Christ may dwell in your hearts through faith. And I pray that you, being rooted and established in love, may have power, together with all the Lord's holy people, to grasp how wide and long and high and deep is the love of Christ, and to know this love that surpasses knowledge — that you may be filled to the measure of all the fullness of God.*

Superficially Sick

Some people are financially rich but spiritually poverty-stricken. Some gain riches, fame and fortune, but that is the only prosperity and abundance they know. The enemy of this world wants us focused on what's seen. He wants our eyes on the fleeting tangible prizes of life, not the eternal promises that only come from God. Riches can put the finest clothes on a sick body, but they can't buy healing.

> *Let's ask God to lead us in being spiritually prosperous. Let's ask Him to help us be better stewards of our spiritual treasures. Some of the poorest people are spiritual millionaires, and some of the richest are spiritually starving. Seek God and gain all.*

Matthew 16:26 - *What good will it be for someone to gain the whole world, yet forfeit their soul? Or what can anyone give in exchange for their soul?*

Proud Purpose

Many people have a special admiration for others they themselves feel unworthy of. Acknowledge your gifts and talents. It's not arrogant to know that you are a wonderful masterpiece full of potential and promise. Arrogance is thinking we are the only ones that are amazing and it causes us to minimize and disregard the excellence in others.

Confidence and self-assurance is knowing God made you in His image and He doesn't make mistakes. It's knowing you may not be like everyone else, but you are still wonderful and uniquely created for greatness. You are a masterpiece. Acknowledge your greatness today and encourage the greatness in others.

Let's ask God to deliver those who don't know their worth. Don't compare your race to others because you have your own lane to run in.

---

1 Corinthians 9:26 *Therefore I do not run like someone running aimlessly; I do not fight like a boxer beating the air.*

You're God's Priority

If we would ever get the true revelation that God is able, we would reach heights beyond our imagination. Sometimes we get so caught up in the sight of a thing that we lose focus on the infinite power available to us. Some feel like God is only interested in the big issues of their lives and try to pick the battles they choose to fight on their own.

God is the God of all things, not just some things. He's not like man. He doesn't put us on the back burner, as if we were not important enough or rich enough or are the last priority on the list of the dignified. He doesn't triage us, as if our needs are of least importance. He is always available and always able.

> Let's ask God to manifest His power in our life issues. Let's ask Him to forgive us for doubting He is able to do exceeding and abundantly above what our limited minds can fathom.

Ephesians 3:20 - *Now to Him who is able to do exceedingly abundantly above all that we ask or think, according to the power that works in us.* (NKJV)

He Wants Your Heart, Not Your Brain

The more we realize God needs less of us to get more of us, the more intimate our relationship with Him will become. Many times people get caught up in the intellectual history and theology of knowing God, but God is not impressed with our knowledge and intellect. He wants our hearts not our brains.

Being able to quote every scripture and recite the paths Jesus trod is not our path to eternity. Even the enemy can recite scripture. Knowing only the letter of God's Word is not the same as having the Spirit of His Word. His Word is not a textbook to be studied, as if we were trying to get an A in a class. God's Word is a living Word that is to be ingested to fill our entire being.

Let's ask God to lead us out of the superficial and into the supernatural through personal revelation of His Word and promises.

2 Timothy 3:7 - *always learning but never able to come to a knowledge of the truth.* (NKJV)

The Phantom Fight

Self-control is not always easy, but it's always possible. When our flesh wars against our spirit, we just have to dig deeper. We have to dig past the emotion, past the anger, past our natural inclinations, past our pride and past our impatience. It's easy to fly off with our mouth and hands, but hard to harness the evil that lurks to distract our purpose and kill our witness.

Some waste hours, days, months and years replaying a hurt or offense in their minds, as they plot a big comeback or revenge tactic. Many times, while we are pondering revenge, the one who inflicted our pain in the first place is moving forward. Stop fighting a phantom.

> **Let's ask God to heal those who are obsessed with revenge, pain, anger and unforgiveness. Let's ask Him to avenge, vindicate, restore and comfort the wrongfully wounded. Your enemies don't need your revenge; they need your prayers. God will handle the rest — in ways you never could. The battle is not yours. It's His.**

Romans 12:19 - *Do not take revenge, my dear friends, but leave room for God's wrath, for it is written: "It is mine to avenge; I will repay," says the Lord.*

Leave The Pity Party

Some may be at a point in life where they are feeling sorry for themselves because life seems to have dealt them a bad hand. It can seem like things always work out for others in life, while some are feeling as though their lives are full of chaotic highs and lows. We all may have been there at some point in time, and it may be you today.

We all have different paths and lessons to learn in order to live in the greatness God has ordained for our lives. God knows what we need in order to be who we need to be. Don't let the process break you. In all you go through, God is our everlasting Anchor. No matter how the cards seem to be falling for you, God is our Game hanger, Favor Finder, Purpose Pusher and Destiny Director.

Let's ask God to crash our pity party and order our steps through the storms we encounter. Your thunder has purpose.

2 **Corinthians 4:16-18** - *Therefore we do not lose heart. Though outwardly we are wasting away, yet inwardly we are being renewed day by day. For our light and momentary troubles are achieving for us an eternal glory that far outweighs them all. So we fix our eyes not on what is seen, but on what is unseen, since what is seen is temporary, but what is unseen is eternal.*

See also Romans 10:9-13

The Enemy of Passive Purpose

Being passive about your purpose will delay your destiny. Days become weeks and weeks become years, so let's examine our mission today. It's time to delete the destiny distractors. Is it social media, bad company, a toxic relationship your flesh keeps holding on to, or is it your fear of failure? You will never know how great your victory is until you are willing to face defeat. You don't know the outcome until you try. The only failure is not trying.

When you try, you may win and, if not, at least you will know it's time to go back to the camp and work harder and pray more strategically.

Let's ask God to renew our strength and faith today. Let's ask Him to bind the distractor of His purpose in us. Sometimes we just need to be delivered from self. Go forth today. You were not created to peddle backward, even though you can.

2 Timothy 1:7 - *For the Spirit God gave us does not make us timid, but gives us power, love and self-discipline.*

The Revelation of the Resurrection

Jesus became a captive so we could be free. He carried every sickness to the cross so we could be healed. He became confusion so we could have peace. He bore every curse and shame so we could be blessed, liberated, righteous and free. He died so we could live, and He rose again with all power so we could rise. That same resurrecting power that raised Him is free and available to us.

Let's take the time to reflect and ask ourselves: what are we doing with the price He paid? What are we doing with the power that's available to us? He didn't die to stay on the cross.

> Let's ask God to lead us in speaking, doing, living and sharing the liberating power that delivered us from ourselves. Let's ask Him to deliver us from routine religiosity so we can get the true revelation of resurrection. Let's die to self so we can rise in Him.

Daniel 12:2 - *Multitudes who sleep in the dust of the earth will awake: some to everlasting life, others to shame and everlasting contempt.*

John 11:25-26 - *Jesus said to her, "I am the resurrection and the life. The one who believes in me will live, even though they die; and whoever lives by believing in me will never die. Do you believe this?"*

Romans 10:9-10 - *If you declare with your mouth, "Jesus is Lord," and believe in your heart that God raised him from the dead, you will be saved. For it is with your heart that you believe and are justified, and it is with your mouth that you profess your faith and are saved.*

Overcoming Your Wilderness

If Jesus was tempted, who are we to think we won't be? In His wilderness, He overcame through steadfast prayer, fasting and faith in who He knew God was. Our wilderness is anything that comes in opposition of who God is, who He says we are and who He wants us to be.

Anything that leads you in the opposite direction of progress is a wilderness. Anything that tries to tantalize your flesh yet reject, neglect and vex your spirit is a wilderness. The thing that seems right to your eyes, but you know is wrong in your heart and soul is a wilderness. When it comes to marriage, that outside person trying to be that outside answer to your inside problem is a wilderness. That quick money fix, which won't lead you to being a good financial steward, is a wilderness. That thing trying to trigger you out of character is a wilderness.

> Let's ask God to lead us through and out of our wildernesses. Let's thank Him for the wilderness experience because the wilderness is where our faith is exercised like any other muscle and becomes stronger. Let's ask Him to strengthen us where we feel weak and hopeless because in that place, He is strongest. Let's overcome the wilderness by overcoming self.

Luke 4:2 - *Where for forty days he was tempted by the devil. He ate nothing during those days, and at the end of them he was hungry.*

2 Corinthians 2:11 - *In order that Satan might not outwit us. For we are not unaware of his schemes.*

2 Corinthians 12:9-10 *But He said to me, "My grace is sufficient for you, for my power is made perfect in weakness." Therefore*

I will boast all the more gladly about my weaknesses, so that Christ's power may rest on me. That is why, for Christ's sake, I delight in weaknesses, in insults, in hardships, in persecutions, in difficulties. For when I am weak, then I am strong.

Author Contact Information

If this book has blessed you, you may contact the author directly at the following email address:

risingabovetherubbishkah@gmail.com

www.ingramcontent.com/pod-product-compliance
Lightning Source LLC
LaVergne TN
LVHW011203080426
835508LV00007B/578